BUCKET
~ TO ~
GREECE

Volume 7

V.D. BUCKET

All names have been changed to spare my wife embarrassment.

Editor: James Scraper

Proofreader: Pamela Cleasby

Cover: German Creative

Interior Format: The Book Khaleesi

Other Books in the Bucket to Greece Series

Bucket to Greece Volume 1

Bucket to Greece Volume 2

Bucket to Greece Volume 3

Bucket to Greece Volume 4

Bucket to Greece Volume 5

Bucket to Greece Volume 6

Bucket to Greece Collection Vols 1-3

Chapter 1

An Almost Fatal Encounter

"What on earth are you doing creeping about down there on the ground, Victor? It's not even light yet," Barry exclaimed, his tone conveying weary irritation. "Do you know how close I came to walloping you round the head with this frying pan? I could have done you a lethal injury."

As I peered through the impenetrable gloom, Barry appeared as nothing more than an indistinct silhouette. A jagged flash of lightning cast a fleeting glow over the garden, giving form to Barry's nebulous figure, an outstretched arm wielding the improvised weapon, frozen mid-motion. Apropos of nothing, the Greek word for fratricide, *adelfoktonia,* flashed through my mind and I rather absurdly pondered if the Greek language had a dedicated word pertaining to the murder of one's brother-in-law. It struck me as unlikely since I couldn't even conjure up such a specific word in the English language.

"I was just..." My words were drowned out by an ominous clap of thunder. Huddled on the ground, I almost lost my balance, brushing against something slimy as I righted myself, narrowly avoiding plunging into the murky depths of the weed infested ecological pond. Losing my grip on the bucket, the lid came ajar, its captive contents releasing a pungent odour as they sprang to freedom. Another bolt of lightning revealed the mass of squirming frogs at my feet in all their repulsive glory. Pushing myself upright, I gave my leg a vigorous shake, dislodging a random amphibian that had made its dash for freedom up my pyjama bottoms.

"Seriously, Victor, frog rustling? That takes the biscuit. If you wanted to study their secretions you only had to ask," Barry reprimanded, his anger at being disturbed by an intruder before first light perfectly understandable.

"I'm not actually plundering your pond, Barry…" The rest of my sentence was cut short as the brooding sky grumbled. The deluge hit, the shock of the downpour comparable to a bucket of water being unceremoniously dumped on my head. Wishing I'd had the fore-sight to pair my pyjamas with wellies rather than socks and sandals, I made a frantic dash for Barry's back door, fervently hoping that the squelching sensation beneath my feet had nothing to do with squashed frogs.

A loud thud accompanied the power going off. Barry's frustrated cry of "Blasted cat" led me to surmise he had tripped over Cynthia's vile feline in the sudden darkness. The damp and bedraggled creature had darted into the house to escape the downpour. No doubt its nightly prowl through the village in amorous pursuit of defenceless strays to ravish had been abruptly cut short by the storm, the atrocious weather putting a damper on Kouneli's libidinous antics.

Reappearing in the kitchen, Barry grimaced, rubbing his shin. "Where did I put that flash-light?" he muttered, adding, "Watch where you're shining that thing, Victor," as I retrieved my torch from my pocket.

Chucking a tea towel in my direction, Barry said, "Use this to get dry; I'm not groping around in the dark for something more suitable." Fumbling about by the sink he filled the kettle, tutting in irritation when he remembered the electric was off, delving blindly into kitchen drawers in search of candles.

"I'll pop the *briki* on the gas camping stove," I volunteered, sniffing the tea towel to check it wasn't too grungy before giving myself a good rub down. Fortunately Cynthia appeared to take tea towel hygiene seriously; she had obviously paid attention when I lectured her on the importance of selecting the boil wash setting on the washing machine.

Soaked to the skin, I was in desperate need of a hot beverage. With the coffee bubbling away in the *briki,* I wrung out my socks and the hem of my pyjama bottoms, the torchlight reflecting the puddles of water on Cynthia's clean kitchen floor.

"It's a bit early even for you," Barry complained, the flickering light from the candles casting shadows on his bleary eyes. "I know you were keen on the frogs breeding but there was no need for you to bung them a bucketful of likely mates."

"I was returning your frogs, not introducing them to promiscuous toads," I countered, struggling to grasp how Barry could imagine I had developed a strange interest in frog procreation.

Barry stared at me blankly: it was still too early for him to grasp my meaning. "So you're saying you were putting my frogs back into the pond?"

"That's right; they turned up as bold as brass in my outdoor bubble bath last night, totally ruining the ambiance of my nocturnal spa, I might add. I was simply returning your property. A bit of gratitude wouldn't go amiss."

Barry was clueless how close I'd come to giving in to temptation and turning his frogs into a garlic rich dish of 'cuisses de grenouilles,' that's fancy French frogs' legs for any gastronomic ignoramuses. I had only resisted my creative culinary urges when I realised I would never persuade Marigold to overcome her aversion to eating the Gallic treat. I couldn't even pass *vatrachpodara* off as a traditional Greek delicacy of our region since the dish is only a local speciality in Ioannina, the capital of Epirus. Barry really should thank me for returning his frogs with a full complement of limbs still attached.

"How do you know they came from our pond?" Barry demanded, clearly burying his head in the sand.

"Call it an educated guess, Barry. Whilst I didn't exactly line them up for an identity parade, I followed my hunch. You have the only ecological pond for miles; where else would they spring from?"

"It's a bit early to cope with your witty sarcasm, Victor."

"I've been tossing and turning for hours knowing Marigold would have a fit if she finds an infestation of frogs in our garden. You know how squeamish your sister gets. Can you imagine the screaming-habdabs she would have if a toad popped up in the bed?" I said. "I decided I might as well make an early start rounding them all up and discreetly returning them to your pond."

"And it didn't occur to you to wait until daylight? You could have landed yourself with the reputation of a peeping Tom sneaking around in the dark with that oversized bucket."

"I thought they may be a tad tricky to catch, I'm not exactly experienced in chasing after frogs," I pointed out, my expertise in local wildlife rather limited to chickens, cats, tortoises and snails. "I've an early start repping on Pegasus and didn't want to chance leaving any random frogs to scare the life out of Marigold, not to mention they could have been toast if they got into the chicken run."

Admittedly, I was a tad clueless if live frogs are actually a delicacy that appeals to chickens; my brood are notoriously unfussy in their eating habits, indiscriminately snacking on any random grasshopper, slug or worm that happens into pecking range. I wouldn't put it past them to greedily devour the odd frog that jumped into their compound.

"I can only imagine Cynthia's hysterics if your rooster decided to make a tasty snack of her precious pond dwellers," Barry chortled, wincing as he took his first sip of Greek coffee. "I'll never fathom how the Greeks can stomach this strong sludge, I'm much happier with a mug of instant or a nice cold *frappé*. Shouldn't it be getting light by now?"

"Not much chance of any light filtering through those low hanging storm clouds," I said, noting that the mountain mist and the driving rain completely obscured the distant view of the sea. "Pass me your mobile, Barry. I want to ring Captain Vasos; I doubt he'll be able to take the boat out in this weather."

"It could well be clear blue skies and calm seas up in town," Barry astutely observed. It was quite remarkable how the weather could differ quite drastically on the other side of the mountain.

I had no intention of suffering an unnecessary drive up to town if there was any likelihood of the Lazy Day boat trip being cancelled due to inclement weather. Thus far during my repping spell, I had suffered two aborted trips on Pegasus: on the first occasion, Vasos, still somewhat under the influence of the previous night's *ouzo*, had recklessly ignored the weather report threatening choppy waters. Rashly pushing forward through the swell, Pegasus was soon tossed around like a cork on the waves, the tourists clinging perilously to the railings and hurling over the sides, their miserable condition exacerbated by the thorough drenching they suffered from the sea spray.

The customer satisfaction surveys would likely have been most uncomplimentary if the rather green passengers hadn't been too shaken to hold a pen. On the second occasion, Vasos soberly decided dangerous waters lay ahead. Calling off the trip before breaking anchor, he broke open the breakfast *ouzo*, miffed that I had no desire to spend my unexpected free time joining him in a day of raucous carousing.

Although I still struggle with telephone Greek, it isn't too bad attempting to communicate with Vasos via mobile. He deliberately keeps his vocabulary simple, whilst bellowing down the phone line with remarkable clarity. The difficulty would be in actually rousing him at this early hour, a necessity unless I wanted to face a potentially wasted journey. As expected, my first call went unanswered. I imagined Vasos snoring away beneath a festering towel, passed out in the grubby cabin on Pegasus. He often spends the night on the boat during summer rather than drunkenly staggering back to whatever hovel he rents.

"Have you got a busy day ahead?" I asked Barry.

"We're meant to be going through the snagging list at Sherry's place, but since Cynthia is working today I'll have to swerve it to look after Anastasia. We were hoping Kyria Kompogiannopoulou would be free to babysit but she's off to the hospital with her bunions. I hate to let Vangelis down, he won't be too happy when he finds out I won't be there to act as a buffer between him and Sherry." Barry shuddered as he spoke; having been on the receiving end of Sherry's suffocating jolly-hockey-sticks manner, I sympathised with Vangelis. Sherry was definitely best diluted.

"Well, it won't be long until Sampaguita is back to babysit on the days Cynthia is working. Spiros is collecting her from Athens on Thursday," I reminded Barry.

"You don't suppose Marigold might offer to have the baby today?" Barry asked. "The ground might be a bit muddy for pulling weeds in the graveyard."

"That won't stop them sitting around drinking coffee and gossiping though," I said. Marigold took the monthly meetings to beautify the cemetery with her Greek friends most seriously, the local women vying to one-up one another in the quality of their homemade cakes. "How about I take Anastasia if the boat trip is cancelled?" I offered rather impetuously.

"Victor, I could kiss you," Barry blurted, thankfully managing to restrain himself from slobbering all over me.

"And to think you were about to wallop me with a frying pan only half an hour ago," I snorted.

* * *

"Vaso, pos einai o kairos ekei?" I shouted down the phone line three coffees later, asking the boat *kapetanios* what the weather was like there.

"Poios einai aftos?" Vasos grumbled, asking who it was, his torpid tone indicating my call had roused him from an *ouzo* induced coma.

"Ego eimai, Victor," I stated the obvious, thinking surely Vasos would hardly be inundated with early morning telephone calls from English gentlemen grappling with the correct pronunciation of telephone Greek.

"Victor?" Vasos slurred my name, seemingly clueless to my identity.

Rolling my eyes at Barry, I shouted to Vasos that I was the tourist rep, before repeating my request for a weather report. *"O touristikos ekprosopos, pos einai o kairos ekei?"*

"Victor, ena lepto, tha koitaxo," Vasos finally replied when it dawned on him who I was, telling me to wait a minute whilst he went off to look. A dull thud indicated he had slung his phone down while he pootled off to observe the weather. An interminable wait followed, leaving me to speculate that Vasos was paying an early morning call to the on-board water closet

and grubbing around through the squalid mess in the cabin to get his hands on a dog-end. The sound of a lighter flicking and the flush of a toilet at the other end of the line led me to deduce I had missed my calling as a detective.

"O kairos einai kalos alla i thalassa einai trachea. Den vgazoume ti varka simera." Once his coughing fit had somewhat abated, Vasos told me that the weather was good, but the sea was too rough to take the boat out. Relieved to be spared a wasted trip, I was surprised when Vasos extended a hearty invitation to spend the day with him drinking *ouzo* and chatting up women, a generous invitation indeed considering he had been clueless who I was only five minutes ago. I suppose his rather pungent aroma could account for a seeming lack of close drinking buddies. Fortunately Vasos dropped the phone and started snoring again before I was forced to invent an excuse to avoid his company.

"It's beginning to get light at last. You'd best get back and change out of your pyjamas, Victor. You'll be the talk of the village if the locals clock you wandering about in your jim-jams," Barry chuckled.

Chapter 2

Bladders and Bunions

Fortunately the rain had subsided from a deluge to a mere drizzle. A fast running river had spontaneously sprung up; gushing forcefully down from the hill above the olive groves it cut a rapid path through the village square, the water sploshing around Spiros' hearse, coming perilously close to soaking the area reserved for a coffin. Luckily the undertaker was onto it, dashing into the flood water in pyjama bottoms and a grubby white vest.

Dispensing with the usual formalities, Spiros shouted across to me, *"poli vrochi."* Talk about stating the patently obvious; one would need to be as plastered as Vasos to have failed to notice that there had been a lot of rain.

Contrary to Barry's opinion that splashing through the village in my pyjamas would likely attract derisive comments, I was relieved to see that I wasn't the only one out and about in my nightclothes. In addition to Spiros being inappropriately dressed for wading towards the hearse, Tina was throwing caution to the wind by appearing in public without even bothering to throw a dressing gown over a rather frumpy nightdress. I suppose vanity was the last thing on her mind as she hastily dragged a couple of heavy looking sandbags into place to create a barrier to prevent the shop from flooding.

One of the old timer regulars who makes a day job out of drinking Greek coffee and playing *tavli* outside the shop rather brusquely barged past Tina in his haste to grab his usual table, seemingly oblivious that it was sitting in a good foot of water. After claiming his seat he shook out a large pocket handkerchief to dry off his hair, bizarrely leaving it atop his head once he'd given it a good wiping. If I hadn't recognised him as a local, I may have easily mistaken him for an old style hanky-on-the-head wearing British tourist.

With my feet forced into Barry's too tight borrowed wellies, I sidestepped the water sloshing over the cobbles, pausing to admire the brilliant arc of a rainbow on the horizon.

"*Kalimera Victor, eisai kala*?" Guzim called out in greeting from his moped, making no attempt to hide the splutter of laughter spewing from his toothless mouth, taking in my unusual choice of attire for roaming the village and spattering me with water as he revved away through a deep puddle. Silently seething and dripping, not at all appreciative of being the butt of my gardener's juvenile sense of humour, I wiped the excess spray from my head, wishing I had thought up a witty retort to wipe the smile off Guzim's face.

Considering the muddy soaking my pyjama bottoms had received, I doubted they'd be fit for anything but the bin. A wicked thought struck me. I have never known Guzim to turn down any of my hand-me-downs; in fact he goes out of his way to get his hands on them by crying that his wife in Albania eats all his money. If I could convince the gullible Albanian shed dweller that my muddy Marks and Spencer pyjama bottoms were the latest summer fashion back in England, I may well be able to persuade him to make a fool of himself by wearing them to the village taverna. I would gladly lure him to the taverna with the offer of some chips and a drink, and derive great pleasure in seeing the locals mock his appalling fashion sense. Whilst not usually prone to such petty thoughts, I imagined basking in the sweetness of such piffling revenge.

Stepping into the garden, I made a final check of the outdoor bath, keen to ensure that all trace of the intrusive frogs had been eradicated; it wouldn't do for my early morning secret mission to be undone by any lingering telltale frog prints. Satisfied there was no evidence of either frogs or their spawn, I decided to tackle the tub later with elbow grease and Vim.

As weak sunlight began to filter through the clouds, I drew a deep breath of fresh mountain air, the rain having released the intoxicating scent of myriad herbs. Looking around the garden, I noticed the clusters of lilac flowers on the chaste trees drooping under the weight of the heavy watering they'd received. Whilst renowned for its potent properties as a female aphrodisiac, the rather attractive plant has earned itself the soubriquet of monk's pepper since it has the opposite effect on the male libido. Pondering the likelihood of monk's pepper having a similar deleterious effect on frog libido as it does on that of religious friars, I decided to take Cynthia some cuttings to transplant around her ecological pond. If the flowering plant proved tasty to the palate of frogs it may have the desired effect of taking the sap out of their bold friskiness, thus making them less likely to make a repeat visit to my outdoor spa. It was certainly worth a try.

Pleased with my plan, I whistled in admiration as a short-toed eagle soared majestically overhead, swooping down gracefully to the hill behind the house in search of prey. Of course it may have been a lesser spotted eagle rather than a short-toed one: the bird was too far away to discern any spots or make a decisive judgment on the length of its toes. I must confess to being a bit of a novice in the identifying different bird breeds malarkey, forced to feign an interest when Dimitris made the subject the central point of our recent doorstep Greek lesson. I am certainly not enough of an eagle-eyed twitcher to distinguish between species, indeed so ignorant of ornithology that I cannot even appreciate the difference between a common starling and a spotted flycatcher. I imagined that Cynthia would be well up on the subject. Since sinking the ecological pond, I rather suspected she was in danger of morphing into a yoghurt-knitting tree-hugger.

"Victor, the air conditioning in here appears to be on the blink, do try and do something with it," the dulcet tones of my wife screeched from the bedroom as I returned indoors. I was surprised Marigold was already awake; perchance the storm had disturbed her lie-in.

"Worry not my love," I assured her. "There's nothing wrong with the air conditioning that the return of the electric supply won't fix."

"Must you talk in riddles?" Marigold complained.

"The power is out again. Hardly unexpected considering the ferocity of the storm we've just had," I explained. Noticing how hot it was already despite the recent storm, I threw the bedroom shutters open. Shuttered windows are a point of contention between my wife and I. Marigold prefers to sleep with the shutters closed and the air conditioning blasting, no matter how many times I warn her of the health and safety risks of breathing in recirculated air, whilst I favour leaving the windows open in the hope that a natural breeze might waft in. Unfortunately Marigold trumped me in that argument as an open window only encourages a plague of mosquitoes and Marigold abhors waking up in Marmite smeared sheets.

"Did it storm? I must have slept through it." Finally noticing that I was a tad bedraggled, Marigold exclaimed, "Good grief, Victor, look at the state of your pyjamas. You look like an indigent down and out, what on earth have you been up to?"

"Just checking up on the chickens, dear." Admittedly I was less than forthcoming with the truth, but my words were not exactly a falsehood since I had glanced in the direction of the chicken coop whilst checking the bathtub was free of frogs. "I'll go and make you a nice cup of coffee."

"You just said we had no electricity."

"I can do you an *Ellinikos kafe* in the *briki,*" I said. The traditional long-handled Greek coffee pot plonked on top of the gas burner was a lifesaver during the frequent power cuts.

"I do find it a bit sludgy first thing, but I suppose it is better than nothing," Marigold grudgingly accepted.

After bringing Marigold coffee in bed, I jumped in the shower, relieved to cleanse my body of frog secretions and slime of dubious origin. By the time I returned to the bedroom, Marigold had perked up from the coffee, eager to reminisce about the lovely time she'd had the previous evening and what a pleasure it had been to meet a sister-in-law she could so readily relate to.

"Don't let Cynthia catch you saying that," I warned her. "It's likely to put her nose out of joint."

"I rub along perfectly well with Cynthia now that she's no longer living under our roof, but there was never the same instant connection that I felt with Elaine. Cynthia considers it a chore to look round the shops, whilst Elaine was telling me how much she'd like to explore what's on offer in town and check out the latest Greek fashions."

"I'm not sure there's anything particularly Greek about the latest line in Marks and Spencer," I said, teasing Marigold about her favourite quintessentially English venue for a spot of retail therapy. Even though the branch in town lacks a food hall, it is a popular store with any local ex-pats that are bold enough to venture into the centre of town rather than limiting their Greek shopping excursions to the German supermarket, Lidl.

I find it quite hilarious that some of the ex-pats that had settled on the coast would rather fly back to England for any non-grocery related shopping that might otherwise involve them confronting their inability to communicate in Greek in an actual Greek shop. Many fail to even bother getting to grips with the polite "*Milate Anglika*?" meaning "Do you speak English?" Even though it is a phrase I rarely resort to it never ceases to amaze me how many shopkeepers reply to my hesitant Greek in tentative English. I have no idea what gives me away as a foreigner when I have made such efforts to integrate.

"Perhaps we could all enjoy a day out up there together, I'd be glad of the chance to spend more time with Douglas…"

"There's really no need for you and Douglas to tag along, you'd only get under our feet. I can do without you making disparaging noises every time I whip out the credit card," Marigold said bluntly. "I'd certainly prefer a day out in town today rather than pulling up weeds in the graveyard."

"I thought you enjoyed the monthly meetings to beautify the cemetery." I was certainly under the impression that Marigold considered the meetings a prime opportunity to brush up on her Greek language skills and integrate with the village women.

"Well, I do, but I can't say I'm in the mood for it today. I expect the cemetery will be a quagmire of mud after the storm, not to mention I'd prefer not to risk running into Papas Andreas in case Geraldine has come clean with him about that sexually transmitted fellow she's been seeing," Marigold said with a heavy sigh. I suppressed a snort at Marigold's novel way of describing Geraldine's new chap. "And since there's no electricity, I won't be able to rustle up one of my *portokalopitas* to take along, you can never go wrong with an orange sponge. I'm sure that horrible Despina in the shop will be only too happy to let the cat out of the bag if I try to pass off shop bought as homemade."

"I have it on good authority from Vangelis that Athena isn't above passing off shop bought as her own baking too," I said. It was quite amazing what one could achieve with a judicious sprinkling of icing sugar and a paper doily.

"Well, I hope that you're a bit more discreet than Vangelis when it comes to blabbing about our private domestic matters," Marigold said with a withering look.

"I think you know I'm not one for gossip, dear," I reassured her, hoping that Vangelis wouldn't repeat what I'd told him about Marigold's regular subterfuge in the home baked department. I had a hunch that Marigold hadn't the slightest intention of whipping up an orange sponge cake; the electric being off was merely a convenient excuse.

"Shouldn't you have left already for your little boat trip? I know how you hate to be tardy."

"Today's Lazy Day cruise has been cancelled due to rough seas. It worked out quite well really as I was able to step into the breach and offer to look after Anastasia. They'll drop her off shortly."

"You make her sound like an unwanted parcel," Marigold huffed. "I have to say, I'm quite envious. You get to spend the day with our darling little bundle of joy whilst I will be grubbing round in the mud yanking out weeds. You don't fancy swapping?"

"Don't try to drag me into it. Beautifying the cemetery is your commitment, not mine," I said. Just then Marigold's mobile rang, sparing me from any of my wife's well-honed persuasive tactics. I'd seen quite enough of the mud at close quarters during my early morning sneaking around.

"Och ochi." Marigold sighed heavily, elongating her vowels and sounding just like a Greek Sybil Fawlty as she repeatedly drawled the Greek for 'oh no' into her mobile. Whilst not intending to eavesdrop, my ears pricked up when I heard my wife say *"nosokomeio."* At the mention of the hospital I could only assume that the Greek caller must be relaying bad news. However, Marigold's gleeful cry of, "Thank goodness for that," as she ended the call demonstrated the folly of making hasty assumptions. Her sudden cheer left me perplexed. Now that Harold no longer resided in the village, I couldn't imagine Marigold celebrating any other resident needing hospital attention.

"That was Athena on the phone," Marigold volunteered. "The beautifying of the cemetery has been postponed until next week."

"Because of the storm earlier?" I enquired.

"No, Athena has a hairdressing emergency and Kyria Kompogiannopoulou can't make it as she has to go up the hospital with her bladder." I resisted the urge to point out that it would be a tad difficult to make the journey without it.

"I thought it was her bunions that were bothering her," I said. Intercepting Marigold's withering look, I clarified my point. "I had it on good authority her bunions were playing up."

"What good authority?"

"Barry..."

"Honestly the two of you are worse than a couple of gossiping old women. Barry always gets the wrong end of the stick, fancy mistaking her bladder for bunions."

As part of my determined effort to improve my mastery of Greek, I had attempted to memorise a long list of medical complaints, telling myself they may well come in handy if Violet Burke did indeed move into our downstairs storage; after all she is forever complaining about her creaking joints and her swollen feet.

Bizarrely bunions had rather stuck in my mind during my studies. According to my dictionary the word for bunion, *kalos,* was identical to the word for good. I had been unable to clarify this point of vocabulary when chatting with the local Greeks; every time I raised the matter they erroneously thought I was asking if their health was good, a typical Greek obsession. Considering half the inhabitants of the village appeared to be raging hypochondriacs, Violet Burke and her medical complaints should fit in quite well.

I can only surmise that such confusing homographs as *kalos* must come automatically to Greeks. In fairness the confusion is reciprocal: there are plenty of examples of bewildering English homographs to trip up any Greek students of the language. Unfortunately, just as ornithology fails to capture my interest, Dimitris tends to tune out when I raise the topic of homophones, homographs and homonyms, preferring to discuss the dietary requirements of his pig.

"Don't blame Barry; he probably got it from Vangelis, who probably got it from Athena," I said in Barry's defence, thinking that Greek gossip had a lot in common with Chinese whispers. "I must say I find the concept of a hairdressing emergency most peculiar. I suppose one of the villagers is in desperate need of a blow dry after being caught out in the downpour."

"There's no need for sarcasm, Victor, hairdressing emergencies are an actual thing. Tina's niece Thalia has suffered a bit of a botched hair disaster. She's inconsolable and refusing to serve in the shop until it's sorted, you know how self-conscious teenage girls can be."

It eluded me why Marigold should imagine I would have the first clue regarding the temperament of teenage girls. Even during his most hormonal years, before he was publicly out and proud, Benjamin had not exactly been dragging random teenage girls home for parental approval.

"There's no need to roll your eyes like that, Victor, you may think yourself above such trivialities but it won't be long until Anastasia, and perhaps even Tilly and Millie, may turn to us for sage advice in their formative years."

"Let's hope so, dear," I replied, realising that Marigold was talking sense for once.

"Thalia wanted to experiment with going blonde but used the sort of bleach that is only fit for cleaning the toilet. Apparently her hair is falling out by the handful, or she could be pulling it out because it went so disastrously wrong, I couldn't really make head or tail of Athena's Greek."

"So in summation, a hair crisis coupled with Kyria Kompogiannopoulou's bladder means you've got out of weeding in a muddy cemetery today," I said.

"It's nice to know you were paying attention, Victor. Sometimes I think you never listen to a word I say."

Chapter 3

Foot-in-Mouth

The sound of the air conditioner spluttering back to life alerted us to the timely restoration of the electricity supply. It was a huge relief to know the power company had for once sorted the issue so promptly. The previous summer we had endured a torturous forty-hour blackout and been forced to bin the entire contents of the deep freeze, even the cats turning their nose up at defrosted Lidl prawns after they'd been sitting around at stifling temperatures for more than a day.

"How about I whip up some *strapatsatha* for breakfast?" I offered.

"Oh, that does sound tempting," Marigold said, never able to resist the Greek dish of scrambled eggs incorporating fresh tomatoes, chives, and feta cheese.

"I'll just pop down and collect some fresh eggs," I said, hoping Marigold wouldn't question why I hadn't collected them when I was supposedly out checking my brood of cluckers earlier.

The telephone rang before I had chance to head to the hen house. Although a tad wary of answering in case it was *Kapetanios* Vasos announcing the sea had calmed and the boat trip was back on, I nevertheless picked up the receiver. I was delighted to discover the caller was my newly discovered half-sibling Douglas, ringing to say what a delight it had been to get together the previous evening. Whilst I had naturally had reservations about meeting Douglas in case he had inherited any shady traits from our mutual father Vic, my worries had been dispelled after spending time together. It was reassuring to discover that we shared common interests rather than any of the fraudulent criminal tendencies that had led to Vic serving time at Her Majesty's pleasure. From first impressions it seemed that neither of us displayed any noticeable evidence of Vic's rather dodgy genes, although our mutual concern with hygiene may well be an inherited characteristic. It appeared I wasn't the only one to be accused of being a tad obsessive on the subject.

My chat with Douglas was interrupted by Marigold snatching the phone from my hand and shooing me out in the direction of the chicken coop whilst she enjoyed a catch-up with Elaine.

I was pleased to note that my brood was hardy stock, the storm having no discernible negative impact on their egg producing abilities. Presented with an abundant lay, I popped half-a-dozen eggs in the bartering bucket on the garden wall for Kyria Maria, wondering what on earth had possessed my neighbour to leave a rather worn and damp pair of men's trousers in the bucket.

I hazarded a guess that the tatty slacks must have belonged to Papas Andreas; one never knew what Greek priests choose to wear beneath their long black vestments, the design ideal for covering a multitude of sins or fashion faux pas. On occasion I had spotted a pyjama hem flapping out below Andreas' austere outfit, but strictly in the privacy of the neighbouring garden and never in public. I wondered if Kyria Maria was under the misguided impression that I coveted her son's cast-offs or whether she simply hoped I would dispose of them to save her a trip to the village bins. Deciding to pass the reject garment along to Guzim, since he is notoriously unfussy about the state of his appearance, I tossed the trousers through the gap in the fence surrounding the garden shed.

Returning to the kitchen, I discovered Cynthia waiting impatiently for Marigold to get off the telephone so she could hand over the baby with appropriate instructions for her care.

"Sorry Cynthia, that was my new sister-in-law Elaine, she's such a delight. Oh you've brought the baby, let me give her a cuddle. Oh yes, you look so cute this morning, my darling." Marigold trilled.

Cynthia and I both perked up at Marigold's unexpected compliment, until Marigold tutted, "I was speaking to the baby, not to you two."

"Victor, it's so good of you to offer to have Anastasia. Are you sure you don't mind and that you will be able to cope okay?" Cynthia said.

"I think I can manage to look after one very small baby for the day," I assured the anxious mother.

I was rather taken aback when Marigold piped up.

"Victor is perfectly capable, Cynthia; he did his fair share in raising Benjamin you know. I don't think you need to worry yourself unduly about Victor being too much of an influence. It's only for one day after all."

"Oh, I didn't mean to suggest..." Cynthia's words trailed off. She was clearly worried she'd put her foot in it.

"Do lighten up, Cynthia, I was simply teasing. Mind you, I can imagine Anastasia regurgitating bacteria and pathogen as her very first words if Victor was to look after her full time," Marigold laughed.

"At least I don't coo over her with infantilising baby talk," I fired back.

"Well, she is an infant, Victor. Only you would expect a three-month old to have swallowed a dictionary." Letting the subject drop, Marigold changed tack. "I must say that Elaine seemed very laid back for such a successful businesswoman, didn't you think, Victor?"

Cynthia shuffled uncomfortably. Rolling my eyes at Marigold's rather tactless comparison of her two sister-in-laws, I hoped that she wouldn't go full foot-in-mouth by suggesting Cynthia follow Elaine's diet plan to shift the last of the baby weight. It was clearly evident to my eyes that Marigold's words had triggered Cynthia's jealous streak. I had witnessed Cynthia's green-eyed tendency before: it raised its ugly head when Barry paid too much attention to Litsa, even though the octogenarian widow who doted on Barry was clearly no competition for his affection.

"Well, I do appreciate you having the baby. Of course I know Anastasia is in capable hands," Cynthia said, only her wobbling lips betraying her hurt feelings at Marigold's tactlessness. "It's lucky that the tourist trip on Pegasus was cancelled so that you could step in. Mind you, I'm sure to be left dealing with the fallout of tourists demanding refunds and complaining about missing the cruise. You know how popular it is."

"At least they won't litter the customer satisfaction surveys with negative comments," I pointed out.

"Since you won't need the Punto to drive to

town, I suggested to Elaine that the two of us drive up for the day to have a browse round the shops," Marigold said. Knowing full well that Marigold was incapable of browsing without flashing my credit card, I inwardly groaned. "I just need you to drive down to the coast and pick up the family, Victor. I assured Elaine you'd be delighted to host Douglas and the twins up here for the day."

"That sounds like an excellent plan," I agreed. "I'm sure the girls would love to see the goats and sheep in Panos' fields, far more educational than spending the day on the beach. In fact I may even bring the twins round to examine the frogs in your ecological pond, Cynthia."

"But the baby…" Cynthia interjected.

"Don't worry; I will wheel Anastasia along in her pram. She's sure to adore the extra attention from the twins."

"I've been wondering if there's any family relationship between Anastasia and the twins. Since we are aunt and uncle to all three girls, I expect that makes them rather loosely related," Marigold said.

"I'm not sure that family trees technically work along those lines," I said, though Marigold had certainly given me something to ponder:

my new found family history was most decidedly complicated. "Now, have I got time to knock up the *strapatsatha* before I drive to the coast or will you and Elaine be splurging on breakfast out in town?"

"I rather think your *strapatsatha* will set me up nicely for the day, darling," Marigold practically cooed, delighted I had so readily fallen in with her plans for our day. "Oh, are you off, Cynthia? Have a lovely day at work and try not to worry about the baby, it would be most unlike Victor to wheel her out somewhere and forget where he's left her."

Chapter 4

Victor's Day Care Centre

"Don't worry, Victor, I'll be sure to remember to pick up a suitable hat for your mother to wear to the christening," Marigold promised as she and Elaine settled themselves into the Punto.

"Just don't go buying something too tasteful, you know how mother's millinery style leans to the flamboyant," I advised. Recalling the lime green monstrosity she had sported for Barry's wedding, I added, "You should be on the right track if you think along the lines of plastic fruit, the more realistic the better."

"Really Victor, when did you become such an expert on women's fashion?" Marigold laughed. "I'll be sure to choose something to make Violet stand out. If the shops don't have any fruity hats, you'll just have to improvise with a few chicken feathers.

Douglas and I waved our wives away before joining my recently acquired six-year-old twin nieces in the garden. Tilly and Millie had taken an instant shine to the baby; in turn Anastasia seemed fascinated by these two miniature people, gurgling happily, her eyes following their every playful move. Douglas had explained that he and Elaine hadn't intentionally lumbered their offspring with cheesy rhyming names. They had more formally named them Matilda and Millicent after some aged aunts on Elaine's side who happened to also be twins. Douglas laughingly confided that the brown-nosing had been a deliberate move in the hope that the elderly spinster twins might bequeath any inheritance that was up for grabs to Elaine, rather than to the local cat charity. I wasn't surprised that the diminutives had stuck; after all Douglas was constantly urging me to address him as Duggie whilst addressing me as Vic, a diminutive I particularly abhor.

"It's so much cooler up here than down on the coast," Douglas said approvingly. He was still a tad pink round the edges from his first day in the Greek sunshine. "I'm not really a big fan of the beach. I tend to burn and peel when I expose my skin to the sun."

"You must never venture out without slapping high-factor sun cream on liberally," I said, slipping naturally into the role of an experienced elder brother doling out invaluable advice. Douglas raised a wry eyebrow in amusement, his attention transfixed on my own reddened forehead and peeling nose. "Much more sensible to keep the children out of the sun during the heat of the day and then let them loose in the sea late afternoon, like the Greeks do."

"It's very good of you to put up with us for the day, I'm afraid that Elaine rather steamrolled Marigold into a girls' day out," Douglas said apologetically.

"Nonsense, Marigold was only saying she would love a day out with Elaine even before you telephoned this morning," I assured him. "And it gives us the chance to become better acquainted."

"You've a lovely place here, Victor, very tranquil, and the views are breath-taking. The village seems quite charming. Can we take a walk around it and explore, if it's not too much trouble?"

"Whatever you want, we have the whole day in front of us and you are on holiday after all," I said. Effectively we were trapped in Meli since Marigold had requisitioned my wheels. There were certainly occasions when I regretted my insistence that my wife get to grips with driving in Greece.

"We were lucky to get that last minute package over. Elaine had us booked into some fancy villa on the Amalfi coast. Knowing how much I wanted to get to know my new-found brother, she cancelled it, so we could come to Greece instead. She didn't even bat an eyelid over losing the deposit."

"I'm glad she changed the arrangements," I said, turning away to hide my guilt when I recalled how close I'd come to fobbing Douglas off with some lame excuse to avoid meeting up. By rearranging their holiday plans, Elaine had demonstrated that she was a thoughtful wife, putting her husband's wishes first. "Neither of our wives could have expected strange siblings to crawl out of the woodwork when they married us…I mean strange as in unknown, not strange as in peculiar."

"Oh, Elaine knew that Vic had a habit of spreading his seed rather indiscrimately. Naturally, I filled her in about Terry and Jimmy before we got engaged," Douglas said. "If anything it was more of a surprise to discover how normal you are, rather than that you actually exist. Elaine took a lot of reassuring that you weren't another vulgar oik like Terry, particularly as I told her that you bear such an uncanny resemblance to him."

"I think the resemblance is rather superficial," I protested.

"Oh I didn't mean to insult you, Vic…"

"Victor," I corrected.

"You are much better preserved than Terry; it's obvious that his seedy lifestyle is beginning to catch up with his looks. So how did Marigold take the news that you have three half-brothers?"

"Considering that she took on an abandoned orphan who had been left in a bucket at the railway station, she took the news of my siblings remarkably well. Of course she had already adapted to the shock of my absconded mother tracking me down and turning up in Greece unannounced."

"Blimey, she just turned up on your doorstep?" Douglas winced.

"Like a Burke from the blue, as I like to quip." Snorting with laughter at my little joke, Douglas was clearly on the same wavelength as me, humour-wise. "I'd had an inkling she was going to put in an appearance when I heard she'd been trying to track me down in Manchester, but it was still a shock to the system."

"I can imagine," Douglas nodded.

"And without sounding harsh, Violet Burke would hardly be one's first choice if one was browsing through a mail-order catalogue to select the ideal mother. There's no denying she is a formidable and bossy woman, not to mention a tad rough around the edges. Still, I cannot deny that she's grown on me; I rather admire her pragmatic approach to life and the way in which she hasn't allowed life's hardships to wear her down," I confided.

"I'm lucky my mum wasn't forced down the bucket route, it would have broken her heart if she'd had to give me up," Douglas said.

"My first impression of Vi was that she was the type that would give away her offspring without a blink of the eye. As I've got to know her, I have come to realise her stoicism on the matter is just a front," I said, recalling how she had jacked in her job at the munitions factory to spare me from coming out yellow. "She does have a heart; she just does a good job of hiding it beneath that ample and very solid bosom of hers."

"I couldn't help noticing there was a bit of a physical resemblance between your mother and Barb Foot. Vic must have strayed from type when he took up with my mother; in contrast to that pushy pair she's much more prim and proper."

"And the one who had Vic's other son, Jimmy. Did she break the mould too?" My curiosity was piqued.

"Joyce. Barb Foot had her pegged to a tee when she described her as all fur coats and no knickers; a looker but terribly common, she must have fitted in well in the prison visiting room. It's funny how Terry and Jimmy have both inherited Vic's philandering ways whilst we are both happily married."

Our conversation was interrupted by the girls' excitedly clamouring to go off and see Panos' goats. Since the sun was now operating at its usual summer strength, I imagined that most of the surplus water that had inundated the village earlier would have evaporated in the heat. Agreeing it was an excellent idea, I insisted everyone top up their sun screen before the off. Duly protected, we were just heading out when Dina intercepted me at the garden gate, practically ramming the pushchair containing Nikoleta into my shins. Clearly frazzled by something, Dina dispensed with the usual prolonged greetings, simply asking me for an urgent favour.

"Chreizomai ti voitheia sas, akousa oti fylakes simera, boreis na pareis kai ti Nikoleta," Dina cried, wringing her hands frantically.

For Douglas' benefit I translated Dina's request. "Dina needs my help; she heard I was babysitting today and needs me to take Nikoleta too. That's her granddaughter."

As soon as I'd spoken, I marvelled that it must already be all round the village that I was taking care of Anastasia today. Things must be incredibly dull if the villagers couldn't find anything a tad more exciting to gossip about. Dina spoke again, apologising for asking me to help out at short notice. I cut her off before she could offer an explanation as to why she needed my help, telling her that no explanation was necessary. Dina was not one to take advantage by asking for help unless she needed it.

"Pigaine, pigaine, o engonos sou einai se thesi mazi mou," I urged Dina to go, assuring her that her granddaughter was in capable hands with me. Dina threw her arms around me, hugging me in gratitude. Scuttling away at speed, she called back over her shoulder, *"Kpatiste tin tyligmene oste na min kryosei."* As Dina hurried away I once again translated for Douglas' benefit, telling him she had instructed me to keep the baby wrapped up so that she wouldn't catch a deathly chill.

Shaking his head at such a preposterous idea, Douglas whistled. "A chill. There's not much chance of that in these temperatures."

Rolling my eyes, I explained, "It's a Greek thing." Fortunately Douglas didn't press me to expound the point since the concept of swaddling babies in summer was one I was still struggling to get my head round.

The two of us looked down at the two babies we had been left in charge of. The difference in presentation was quite stark. Propped up in her pram, little Anastasia's chubby bare legs wriggled freely below a sleeveless light cotton dress, a matching sun hat protecting her head. In contrast, Nikoleta was kitted out in a knitted onesie, her curls hidden by a woolly hat, over-sized ear flaps securely tied in place beneath her cute little chin. As an extra precaution, Dina had piled on the heavy blankets: perish the thought that the slightest draught might penetrate the layers.

"I think I've missed my calling as a day-care centre," I quipped.

"The more the merrier," Douglas said cheerily, grabbing the handle of Nikoleta's pushchair without being asked, completely unfazed by the addition of another baby.

Chapter 5

A Ferocious Guard Dog

It was hard to believe that the village had been practically underwater only hours earlier, yet pleasant to note that the cobbles had been washed clean of their usual coating of Saharan red dust. The only hint that a storm had blown through the peaceful lanes was the exceptionally strong scent of fresh wild mint, thyme and garlic suspended in the air, and the delectable lushness of the vegetation. The olive farmers would certainly appreciate the abundant downfall. Bursting with energy, the children skipped along cheerfully as we made our way up the rough track that led to Panos' fields, excited at the prospect of rubbing noses with real live goats.

"Yassou, Victor, eisai kalytera tora?"

I looked around in confusion, trying to fathom where the voice hailed from that asked me if I was better now. There was no one in sight. I jumped two feet in the air when Giannis suddenly popped up out of nowhere on the other side of the hedgerow, his unruly dark locks all askew. A backdrop of colourful bee boxes provided the motive for his presence. Hopefully my still sun reddened complexion hid my blushes. I hadn't run into the handsome bee man since the unfortunate incident when I had passed out and been hosed down at Poppy's house. It was only natural to feel more than a tad embarrassed that I had been attended by a veterinarian rather than a human doctor.

Fortunately it dawned on me that even if Giannis was tactless enough to raise the subject, I would be spared further humiliation since Douglas wouldn't have a clue what he was talking about. I could only imagine the twins' hoots of laughter if they discovered that a veterinarian had turned his hosepipe on Uncle Bucket. Perchance it will make for an amusing anecdote once I am in my dotage, but for now the less said on the subject the better.

"Pou pas?" Giannis asked where we were going.

"Sta katsika tou Panou," I replied, telling him we were going to see Panos' goats, adding that the children were excited to see the animals, *"Ta paidia einai enthousiasmena pou vlepoun ta zoa."*

"Malista, fere tous na doun ta kounelia mou argotera," Giannis said, telling me to bring them to see his rabbits later.

"Isos." My reply of 'perhaps' was intentionally non-committal. I was not sure how I would go about explaining to the children that the cute bunnies were being bred as food rather than adorable pets. It may be less traumatic to simply introduce them to Doruntina, Guzim's pet rabbit, since the Albanian shed dweller would never dream of eating his cuddly bedfellow.

The twins were almost giddy with anticipation as the melodic tinkling of bells heralded our arrival at Panos' field. I was delighted to see that the welly wearing farmer was on hand to invite us onto his land: even though I consider Panos a good friend, my law-abiding nature still made me flinch a tad at the prospect of illegal trespass. After cooing over both babies, Panos encouraged the twins to approach his animals. Panos' flock represented fine specimens in rude health, a mixture of ornery elders, sprightly mountain explorers and impudent kids. Observing them, I considered one would be hard-pressed to find a more attractive trip of goats anywhere, ranging in colour from white to brown, to a mottled mix. The twins kept their distance from the odd bearded, horned beast eyeing them warily, giggling in delight when Panos scooped up a cute little kid for them to stroke.

With the children's curiosity finally satisfied, Panos invited us to step into his house for a cool drink. Although I was loathe to impose, Panos insisted, refusing to take no for an answer. As he led the way through his yard to the kitchen, Douglas and I made a grab for the children to prevent them from rushing to pet Panos' ferocious guard dog; even securely tied up it appeared to consider them a tasty snack.

Since my expertise in dog breeds is as lacking as my knowledge of ornithology, I was clueless as to what particular brand of canine the enormous shaggy black and grey brute represented; indeed it may even have been black and white, just exceedingly dirty. Keeping my distance, I cowered in fear as the dog growled menacingly, straining against its rope, saliva drooling from its mouth in a most repulsive display of slobber. Even if its ferocious demeanour had not instilled mortal terror in me, I would have still kept my distance, convinced that all manner of dubious germs could be breeding in its filthy, burr matted fur.

"Min fovasai, to Apollo einai ena softie," Panos clucked, reassuring us there was nothing to be afraid of as Apollo was a softie. Belying his words, the dog began barking furiously. My ears pricked up at the familiar sound. Until this moment I hadn't realised that the irritating hound responsible for disturbing my sleep on many a night belonged to Panos. I had often been woken in annoyance by the noisy creature howling at the moon, leaving me tossing and turning. If my telephone Greek wasn't so abysmal, I would probably have made a few desperate late night phone calls to the Greek police in the hope that if they couldn't arrest it for noise pollution they could at least insist that the owner slap a muzzle on it. Too reluctant to make the call, I had instead been reduced to fantasising about canicide as I lay there counting the

proverbial sheep.

Jumping up on its hind legs, Apollo attempted to gnarl through its rope. Firmly instructing the dog to calm down, Panos told me that he needed to go into town to buy a new chain to secure Apollo; the previous night the dog had gnawed through its rope and escaped. Even though he had managed to retrieve Apollo, I was a tad alarmed to notice the precariously frayed state of the rope, fearing the dog may repeat its escape. I asked Panos to let me know when the dog was safely back in chains since I certainly wouldn't feel safe indulging in my outdoor spa if there was the slightest possibility of it chewing its way to freedom and joining me in the bathtub. Even if it restrained from turning me into its dinner, the prospect of its slobbering all over me was too hideous to contemplate. In truth, I would rather suffer another infestation of frogs.

"Ela, echoume ena poto mesa," Panos said, repeating his invitation to come inside for a drink.

Edging tentatively past the guard dog, we passed a pot of something emitting a vile stench, simmering away atop a makeshift barbecue. Recoiling in horror at the prospect of being force fed the contents of the pan, I realised I must fabricate an imaginative excuse to reject any offer of food, even though such a rejection would be a direct snub of Greek hospitality. Noticing my utter disgust triggered by the noxious smell from the pan, Panos dissolved into laughter.

"Victor, afto einai fagito yia ton skylo."

I exhaled in relief as Panos explained the food was for canine rather than human consumption. Entering the house we crowded into the oppressively hot, small dark kitchen. I immediately felt the uncomfortable sensation of sweat dripping down my back.

"Chreiazeste enan anemoskala edo," I said, advising Panos he needed a fan.

"Yiati?" Panos' face was suffused in confused incredulity as he demanded to know why.

"Yiati einai poly zesto edo." Stating the obvious, I told him the fan was needed because it was very hot in here.

"I anemoskala? Victor, eisai trelos," Panos laughed. It was not immediately apparent why Panos was calling me crazy until it dawned on me that *anemoskala* was not only the incorrect Greek word for fan but it was in fact a word I had dragged from the dark recesses of my brain, clueless to its actual meaning.

"Ena lepto," I said buying myself a minute as

I dragged out my convenient Greek to English pocket dictionary and flicked through the pages. No wonder Panos thought I was mad: I had just advised him he needed a rope ladder to cool the place down.

"Chreiazeste enan anemistira," I hastily corrected, this time telling Panos he needed a fan.

Panos practically spat on the floor at such a ludicrous suggestion, proclaiming he would never give house room to one of those disgusting contraptions: everyone knew that indoor fans made one sick.

This was not the first time I had heard a Greek person express such an uninformed opinion. It appeared that my Greek neighbours laboured under the universal misapprehension that fans were so dangerously unhealthy that anyone exposed to such horrible modern contraptions would instantly be stricken down with a fatal dose of pneumonia. Their illogical fear was nothing but an old wives' tale. Ironically many of my Greek friends that live in fear of fans, covet air conditioning, dismissing my repeated warnings that unless the units are maintained in a scrupulously hygienic condition they could provoke an outbreak of Legionnaires' disease.

Panos cracked open a can of Fanta *lemoni* for the twins to share, raising his bushy eyebrows when I declined his offer of a mid-morning *tsipouro* in favour of tap water. Once again, I noted Douglas was happy to defer to the wisdom of his elder brother, heeding my warning that the fiery *tsipouro* would be his undoing.

Panos wasted no time enquiring about Violet Burke, fuelling my suspicion that the farmer was quite taken with my mother. His delight was evident when I informed him that she would be flying into Greece on Thursday. The two of them had forged a somewhat surprising friendship considering they were incapable of communicating in the same language, apparently content to talk at one another despite their mutual lack of comprehension. My mother shared a similar camaraderie with Kyria Maria. The two of them got along swimmingly, rubbing along without any friction if I ignored their demands that I translate. On occasion, I was forced to give in to the pressure to, "Tell me what she is saying," but found the diplomatic way of maintaining the peace was to simply make up some innocuous remarks rather than translating their actual stabs at conversation.

Upon hearing the news that Violet Burke

would be in Meli within days, Panos immediately started finger combing his rather unruly moustache and eyebrows, and muttering he must get a haircut. I tactfully restrained from voicing my opinion that his filthy wellies could do with a good polishing too.

Panos' enthusiasm for Vi's visit reminded me that I really needed to broach the subject of our downstairs storage with Marigold at the first opportunity. No doubt she was at that very moment flashing my credit card in town and devising ways to discreetly sneak bags of new clothing into the back of the wardrobe, practicing her well-used line of, "Really, this old thing, Victor, I've had it forever. Sometimes I think you wouldn't notice if I went out for dinner in a bin bag." If I could catch her in the act of stashing her extravagant purchases out of sight, I wasn't above turning the situation to my advantage.

Revitalised from the refreshments, Panos insisted on raiding his vegetable garden, loading us up with fresh romaine lettuce, spring onions and a huge bunch of dill, using his hands to expressively convey to Douglas how delicious the fresh salad makings were. As we made to leave, Panos pulled me aside, hissing, "*Pes sti mitera sou oti tha tis fero merikes kales patates tiganismatos."* I nodded sagely, suppressing my urge to laugh as Panos told me to tell my mother he would bring her some good frying potatoes. Who said romance was dead? Panos clearly appreciated that the way to my mother's heart was through the chip pan.

Strolling back through the village, Douglas told me a little more about Elaine's successful diet company, explaining one of the thorniest challenges his wife still faced was making salads sexy enough to appeal to desperate dieters who despite their best intentions were still obsessed with chocolate biscuits. The closest many of them had come to an actual salad before embarking on their weight loss journey had been a McDonald's garnish. Douglas explained that even when diet converts reluctantly changed their eating habits, they tended to self-sabotage, ruining a healthy salad by dumping the calorific contents of a bottle of Heinz salad cream or Thousand Island dressing over the greenery.

Pondering Douglas' diet dilemma, I shared my opinion that eating habits were largely ingrained, explaining that Greek people held salads in such high regard that they spoke of them in almost reverential, loving tones. Undoubtedly their demonstrative affection was nurtured by spending their impressionable years in their grandmother's kitchens where they also absorbed the erroneous information that veering too close to a fan would land them in hospital.

Whilst Marigold and I had made an effort to include salads in our Manchester diet, they had only become a daily part of our lives since moving to Meli and being exposed to the influences of the Greek way of life.

Expounding my point, I told Douglas that in my constant endeavours to improve my Greek language skills, I had made a real effort to watch Greek television, often turning it off in frustration at my inability to grasp what the talking heads on the screen were actually saying. It was Barry who had introduced me to the Greek version of 'Survivor', a popular reality television programme he had become quite addicted to back in England. Over the previous winter Barry and I had huddled around the television set, Marigold scoffing at what she considered our indulgence of such low-brow rubbish. Whilst my wife preferred to retire to bed with one of her interminable, exclamation mark littered, moving-abroad books, we were glued to the screen. Barry explained the concept of the programme to me; at first I simply humoured my brother-in-law by joining him, but in no time at all I was hooked, Barry and I high-fiving each other whenever we could translate anything the contestants said.

Noticing that Douglas' eyes were beginning to glaze over in boredom, I got to the point. Barry had told me that the winning team was often rewarded with food treats. In the English version the teams had salivated over rewards of pizza and chocolate cake. In contrast the Greek contestants were intoxicated when they won a food reward of the tomatoes and chicken *souvlaki* they had been craving.

"Ah, I get your point, you are saying it is a cultural thing to get excited at the thought of a tomato," Douglas said.

"Exactly," I agreed.

"So, how do we convince English dieters that there's anything remotely sexy about this?" Douglas asked, waving one of Panos' freshly picked lettuces in my face.

"Let's experiment this afternoon by giving the lettuce a traditional Greek twist," I suggested. "In truth, I have seen grown men practically weep with pleasure at the prospect of tucking into *maroulosalata*."

"What's that?"

"Lettuce salad."

"It will be a miracle if you can make a lettuce enticing," Douglas scoffed. The doubtful smirk was wiped off his face as little Nikoleta leaned forward in her pushchair, attempting to snatch the tempting lettuce out of Douglas' hands. Even at such a tender age the infant clearly recognised the makings of a good Greek lunch. An amusing thought struck me: since Anastasia had British parents but would enjoy a Greek upbringing, I wondered whether it would be the sight of a lettuce or a tin of Fray Bentos steak and kidney that would most excite her once she graduated onto solid food.

Chapter 6

Not at all Squeamish

"What it really needs is Benjamin's magic touch to add some pizzazz," I mused, staring at the rather unappealing bowl of *maroulosalata* that Douglas and I had cobbled together. I imagined my son's talented skills as a professional food stylist transforming the rather unimpressive bowl of limp lettuce into a veritable work of leafy art. Even a generous drizzle of local extra virgin olive oil had done nothing to add the essential wow factor to the bowl of shredded greens, chopped spring onions and dill, leaving it distinctly unlikely to entice chocolate addicts into becoming salad junkies. To add insult to injury, the twins refused to sample the salad, turning their cute little noses up at the oily dressing. They were quite content to munch away on raw carrots, but their refusal to tolerate a drop of olive oil on any vegetables reminded me of Violet Burke's scathing dismissal of the Greek elixir.

Undeterred, Douglas remained enthusiastic about our creative culinary project of adding Greek inspired dishes to Elaine's successful commercial diet plan. He was eager to press on by experimenting with the next healthy recipe on our list, *avgolemono*. This quintessentially Greek lemon chicken soup is revered as a remedy for any ailment in *Hellenic* households in much the same way that traditional chicken soup with matzo balls is regarded as Jewish penicillin. Unfortunately, the twins got the wrong end of the stick and thought I was about to go out and murder one of the chickens to add to the pot.

My reassurances that no live chickens would be sacrificed in the name of *avgolemono* were received with petulant and suspicious glares.

I was left with no other option than to take the girls outside and introduce them to my boozy named brood. If they happened to pipe up how much they liked *raki* and *ouzo* after being in my care, I hoped that their mother wouldn't consider me a disreputable uncle leading her children astray. I would hate for Elaine to lump me in with Terrance and write me off as a bad influence.

With Nikoleta and Anastasia enjoying a midday nap under Douglas' watchful eye, I led the way to the chicken coop, the twins as giddy with excitement as though I had promised them a day at the zoo. The girls chased manically after my prize poultry, determined to catch and hug them. Raki, unable to outrun the twins because of its gammy leg, only managed to extricate itself from a suffocating cuddle with a timely peck. Fortunately for my reputation as a responsible uncle no actual blood was drawn, though I remain unconvinced that the seemingly traumatised chickens derived quite as much enjoyment from the impromptu visit to their pen as the children did.

Kyria Maria popped up on the other side of the garden wall, a rather unpleasant, if convenient, distraction. The sight of the wrinkled old woman clad all in black and brandishing her broomstick appeared to frighten the children a tad; I pondered how they would react if her son was to follow her into the garden. I doubted the children would be used to the sight of a bearded man swanning about in long black vestments.

Sidling over to me for protection, the twins gawped at my neighbour, hissing, "Is it a witch?" Their tactless question made me glad that Maria hadn't managed to pick up any English whilst conversing endlessly with my mother, though on reflection the two of them together did remind me of a gossiping witches' coven.

Maria scuttled away, returning to proudly show off her new pet. Ruining her image of a witch, she held the tortoise, rather than a black cat, aloft, her creased face transformed by a welcoming crinkly smile.

"*Ela, afti einai i helona mou,*" Maria said.

"The *Kyria* is showing you her tortoise," I translated.

"What's it called?" Tilly asked.

"Maria," I told her.

"*Ti?*" Maria's ears pricked up at the mention of her name.

"My neighbour and the tortoise are both

called Maria," I clarified.

"But you said she was called the *Kyria,*" Millie said in confusion.

"*Kyria* is the Greek way of saying Mrs, it is the polite way of addressing one's elders," I explained.

"Like the way Mummy says we have to call you Uncle Bucket and not Vic?" Millie said.

"Exactly," I said, cringing at the diminutive of my name and looking nervously over Maria's shoulder in case her son appeared. It could get a tad confusing if I was called upon to explain why the girls would need to address a bearded man in a black dress as father when he clearly wasn't related to them. Fortunately there was no sign of the priest, sparing me a convoluted lesson in the formally correct way of addressing the Greek clergy. It occurred to me that Papas Andreas was likely cutting a solitary figure pulling up weeds in the graveyard, no doubt cursing his usual helpers as a bunch of irresponsible heathens, happy to neglect their monthly duties when faced with the infinitely more appealing worldly temptations of hairdressing and shopping for new frocks.

When the children had duly prodded and poked the tortoise, I ushered them back into the house to scrub any salmonella germs off their hands. Using the excuse that I was also babysitting for Dina and Cynthia, I declined Maria's offer to stuff the twins with meatballs and macaroni washed down with Fanta *lemoni,* even though they appeared quite eager to visit the cat free lair of a real live witch. Fortunately the news that my mother would soon be descending on us for another visit served as a suitable distraction, Kyria Maria declaring she must hurry to finish the new cardie she was knitting for Violet Burke. Without giving due consideration to my choice of Greek words, I told Maria that my mother would be touched by such a thoughtful gesture, rather taken aback when she tutted in disapproval, looking me up and down as though I had lost my marbles. It was only later when I had chance to confer with my dictionary that I realised I'd committed yet another language faux pas, telling Maria that my mother was a bit touched in the head. Considering Maria's inexplicable fondness for Violet Burke it was no wonder she'd seemed a tad put out by such a vocal display of filial disrespect.

Unable to tempt the children with a low calorie lunch of *maroulosalata,* I was pleased when they showed suitable enthusiasm for the fresh eggs the chickens had laid that morning, seemingly oblivious until that moment that eggs came out of a chicken's bottom rather than a cardboard egg box. Whilst we tucked into our lunch, Douglas explained to his daughters that I was an expert authority on disgusting germs and nasty bacteria, unleashing a rather unwholesome, indeed rather morbid, interest in the subject. Dipping toast soldiers into runny yellow yolks, the twins listened in rapt fascination as I regaled them with some of the most lurid and colourful tales from my illustrious days as a public health inspector.

Their eagerness to lap up every grisly detail of kitchen gore, from festering foodstuffs erupting in mould to the most outrageous examples of hygiene violations, reminded me of Benjamin's childhood days. He had displayed the same fascination for every disgusting detail of rancid green chicken and scummy sauces. For some reason, I had expected girls to demonstrate more squeamishness, but they lapped up my gruesome descriptions with relish. Recalling that my embellished tales of penny pinching chefs taking leftover chips from the plates of spit happy customers and merrily lobbing them back into the deep-fat fryer had left Benjamin with a lifelong phobia of restaurant chips, I deliberately omitted all mention of the subject.

Even though my tales of kitchen filth appeared to turn Douglas a tad green around the edges, the twins continued to pester me for more foul details. Playing to a rapt audience, I described the effects of salmonella and campylobacter bacteria when they are passed from chickens and tortoises to humans.

"Do you have a really, really big sick bucket, Uncle Bucket?" Tillie giggled.

"Steady on, Vic, we don't want them having nightmares," Douglas remonstrated as I launched into a vivid description of human salmonella symptoms.

"It's never too early to drum in the importance of scouring one's hands," I assured Douglas.

"But the dining table is not really the appropriate setting for delving too deeply into the finer details of diarrhoea and projectile vomit," Douglas tutted.

"Well, it doesn't appear to have put your children off their food," I pointed out as the twins demanded ice cream.

"It's actually a bit worrying the way they aren't fazed by such disgusting details," Douglas said in a worried tone.

"I wouldn't worry unduly. Benjamin was brought up on such tales and it didn't turn him into a serial killer," I reassured him.

"What's a serial killer?" Millie and Tillie piped up in unison.

"Why don't you two girls go and play nicely with the cats whilst Uncle Bucket and I clear the dirty dishes?" Douglas said, deftly changing the subject.

"And then we'll all take a walk to the village shop for some ice cream," I promised as the children ran off to find the cats.

"You do have such delightful children, so well mannered, they are a credit to you," I said, impressed by the way the girls were following their father's instruction to go off and play quietly, without getting under our feet.

"They are in their element here meeting all the animals. They've been badgering me for a new pet for a while, but after that unfortunate incident with the goldfish I wanted to make sure they are responsible enough," Douglas sighed. It didn't escape my notice that he didn't expound on the fate of the aforesaid goldfish.

Since meeting Maria's tortoise and Marigold's cats, the girls had been squabbling over what type of animal they wanted as a pet, and I hadn't even introduced them to Guzim's pet rabbit yet. Douglas had wasted no time in vetoing their impractical demands for a pet goat, whilst Panos' fearsome guard dog had put them off the idea of adopting a puppy.

The peaceful domestic scene of two half-brothers companionably washing the lunch dishes was shattered when two bundles of frothing soapsuds streaked across the kitchen floor, leaving a trial of soapy puddles in their wake. Only their desperate high pitched yowls identified the furiously moving balls of suds as Marigold's pampered domestic felines. The twins followed in hot pursuit, dripping and skidding across the kitchen floor, screeching, "Come back, kitty." Taken aback by this farcically wet intrusion, I momentarily wondered if the storm had returned before recalling the twins had been playing indoors.

Shaking its head violently and soaking Douglas with scattered spray, Clawsome leapt onto the draining board to evade her pursuers, sending Marigold's cut glass salad bowl to the tiled floor where it smashed into smithereens. Catastrophe flung herself at me for protection, covering me in soapsuds.

"Girls, stop," Douglas commanded. "What on earth is going on?"

"We were giving the cats a nice bath..." Tilly began.

"To wash off their nasty zoo bacteria," Millie finished.

"Zoonotic," I automatically corrected before realising there were more important issues at hand that needed addressing. I instructed the twins to, "Stay exactly where you are, this broken glass is a dangerous safety hazard."

Taking charge of the sweeping brush, Douglas adroitly dealt with the myriad shards of broken glass whilst scolding his daughters. "You can't go around tormenting innocent animals. Cats really don't like being washed with soap and water; they prefer to lick themselves clean."

"It's not soap, it's jelly," Millie argued, flaunting a by now almost empty bottle of Marigold's precious Rive Gauche shower gel. It was no wonder my now sudsy shirt made me stink like a perfume counter. I considered that no matter how much my wife adores the cats, she would never waste her expensive scented body wash on the creatures. No doubt the lure of designer scent would only encourage Cynthia's vile tom, making our cats irresistibly attractive to Kouneli if it got wind of them.

"Can we stop having horrible baths and lick ourselves clean like the cats?" Tilly demanded.

"Licking isn't hygienic for humans. It would mean ingesting all manner of muck and bacteria that you may have picked up," I said. "I'm sure you were only trying to help but you shouldn't have tried to wash the cats. They aren't ridden with nasty bacteria; the veterinarian gave them a clean bill of health…"

My lecture was interrupted by sinister strangulated sounds coming from the frothing mouths of both cats. As they began to cough up soapy fur balls, I surmised that attempting to lick off expensive scented soapsuds had not gone down too well with their digestive systems.

"I think we'd better rinse the cats off under the tap before they ingest any more suds," Douglas advised, making a grab for Catastrophe and holding the squirming feline firm in the kitchen sink under the running tap.

"I'll go and grab a towel," I called out, heading to the bathroom, only to be greeted by the sight of complete disarray in the flooded room. Marigold would have kittens if I didn't return the twins' devastating handiwork to pristine order before she returned.

Chapter 7

A Dog Day Afternoon

Peace had finally descended on my rather impromptu day care centre. Dina had retrieved her granddaughter, and the exhausted twins were taking an unexpected siesta on the sofa-bed in my office. Anastasia was sleeping peacefully in the shade, whilst Douglas and I were relaxing in the garden with a nice cup of Earl Grey. Pickles was curled up on my lap purring contentedly, having been mercifully spared an unwanted bath at the hands of the twins. Sipping our tea in companionable silence, we gazed at the rolling hills in the distance, the rather pleasant herbaceous scent of wild chamomile tempting our senses as we relished the quiet. The late afternoon tranquillity was rudely shattered when a clearly hysterical Marigold rushed into the garden, her face a deathly shade of white.

"Victor, you have to come at once, I've killed it. It ran right at the Punto out of nowhere…oh what I have done?" she screeched.

Springing to my feet I advised, "Take a deep breath, Marigold," worried my wife was about to faint from shock. "What do you think you may have killed?"

A nip at my ankles reassured me that Pickles was safe, though somewhat disgruntled at being unceremoniously tipped off my knee.

"I don't know…it was huge. I didn't see it until it was too late, it all happened in a flash. It hurled itself at the car like a creature possessed," Marigold gasped between hyperventilating.

Douglas and I wasted no time in hurrying out to the street where Elaine was crouching down by the side of the Punto, her hovering figure concealing an indeterminate form, bulky and inanimate. Moving closer, I immediately recognised Panos' ferocious guard dog, though since it appeared to be dead it didn't look half as fearsome as it had earlier when it had been straining and slobbering against the confines of its rope. My heart leapt into my throat. I took a deep breath to counter my sense of panic, my first instinct to protect my wife from any unpleasant repercussions.

Clearly the dog was at fault. Having chewed through its restraints, it must have escaped from Panos' yard and into the street where it had indiscrimately attempted to attack the Punto, failing to recognise the superior strength of the moving vehicle. I reflected that it was fortunate that it must have hit the car sideways on, thus sparing the undercarriage considerable damage and an expensive repair job.

"Do you think we should try and give it the kiss of life?" Douglas grimaced.

"Feel free if you like, but I'm certainly not getting that up close and personal with the ugly brute," I replied, my stomach recoiling in disgust at the thought of inhaling a mouthful of foul dog breath. I imagined Apollo's stench would be particularly fetid considering the vile smelling stuff that Panos had prepared to feed it earlier.

"We mustn't let the children see it, it will give them terrible nightmares," Elaine cried out. As she voiced her fears it was a welcome relief to realise I wasn't alone in being consumed by selfish thoughts, more concerned about my wife and my car than some random dead dog.

Unfortunately since Apollo belonged to my friend and neighbour it could hardly be discounted as an entirely random mutt, though I must confess to a certain bias against the soiled mongrel considering how many disturbed nights I had suffered due to its relentless howling. Luckily, I realised that since it was siesta time the village was quiet, the locals no doubt enjoying a post-lunch snooze behind closed shutters. It was doubtful that anyone had noticed Marigold's vehicular homicide, thus suiting the urgent need to dispose of the evidence before the twins encountered it.

"It's a hefty lump of monstrosity and no mistake," Douglas commented, not bothering to temper his words to avoid speaking ill of the dead. "Do you think we can shift it between us, Vic?"

"I would think so, but where will we put it?" I asked, my brain too consumed by the urgency of our predicament to bother correcting my brother's diminutive use of my name.

"It has to be somewhere the children won't stumble across it. We must shield them from the horror or it will ruin their holiday," Elaine insisted. I didn't feel that this was an appropriate time to mention that her children appeared to have a rather morbid fascination with gore and would most likely revel in the scene.

"How about stashing it in our downstairs storage?" Marigold suggested, beginning to emerge from shock.

I recoiled at the very suggestion. It was a terribly hot afternoon and I didn't fancy the filthy dead canine decomposing and festering in my storage space, likely spreading all manner of unhygienic contaminants. Depending on the speed of autolysis the storage area could well end up requiring a thorough fumigation if the canine corpse started to putrefy before we could do something with it. The 'something' we needed to do rather eluded me: obviously the decent thing to do would be to confess to Panos and return the accidentally slain guard dog to him, but the more practical solution may be to remain tight-lipped, dig a giant hole, and bury it under cover of darkness.

"We could hide it in Guzim's shed for now."

I had noticed the Albanian had left the door off the latch when I'd tossed the Papas' trousers over earlier. In fact said trousers would serve as an excellent item to roll the dead dog onto, enabling us to smoothly drag it across the garden; I had no desire to waste a perfectly good car blanket by soiling it with possibly flea infested dog hairs.

Dashing through the garden, I retrieved the discarded trousers and hurried back to the still mercifully deserted street. Between us Douglas and I managed to roll the sizeable bulk of dog onto the trousers which we then used to drag the creature away before any prying eyes could clock what we were up to. It wouldn't do to get a reputation for carrying on in a nefarious manner during siesta time; after all I had a certain reputation to maintain if I wished to retain my good standing amongst the villagers.

It was a stroke of good luck that Guzim had left his shed unlocked. As I opened the door, Doruntina, Guzim's pet rabbit, streaked past me, no doubt making a beeline for my vegetable patch. At least it hadn't broken loose when Apollo was on the prowl; Guzim would be prostrate with grief if the slobbering guard dog had made mincemeat of his beloved rabbit. We duly dragged the shaggy beast into the shed, depositing it on the floor which I couldn't help but notice was almost as filthy as the dog. Douglas and I looked at one another rather askance since this was as far as our improvised plotting had taken us.

"It's not too late to telephone Panos and tell him about the accident. He may well understand that we reacted in haste so that the grisly sight didn't upset the children," I suggested hesitantly, unsure if my Greek language skills were up to the necessary explanations.

"Actually there's a remarkable lack of gore, not even any blood, unless it has soaked into those old trousers," Douglas noted. "I think you should think twice about owning up though, it might land Marigold in trouble with the law. I read some horrible reports about unspeakably vile conditions in Greek prisons after those anoraks got themselves arrested for illegal plane spotting. Do you happen to know what the penalty is over here for accidentally killing a dog?"

"I can't say that I'm up on the subject." Douglas' words made me go weak at the knees. The very thought of Marigold confined in a Greek prison was too unthinkable to contemplate. "I'm sure Spiros would know what the penalty is for canicide."

"Spiros?" Douglas queried.

"The local undertaker."

"Does he do a thriving business in burying dead dogs?"

"No, of course not, but he's a very good friend and the fountain of all local knowledge," I said, wondering if it was wise to involve him or just keep schtum. Whilst I knew Spiros had no time for cats, unfortunately I was ignorant about his views on dogs.

"The hound was clearly dangerous and should have been securely chained up, that frayed rope was a joke. Imagine if it had got its teeth into a child, it doesn't bear thinking about," Douglas shuddered. "Your friend with the goats is the one clearly at fault for not securing his vicious animal properly."

I was completely torn. On the one hand Panos had appeared to be quite fond of his dog; the decent thing would be to let him know about the unfortunate accident. On the other hand Panos should have ensured his dog could not get loose to terrorise the neighbourhood; the shoddy rope he had used had been an open invitation for Apollo to escape, thus putting Marigold at risk. She may well have suffered an injury during the collision between the dog and the Punto. Whilst I dithered over the right thing to do, Douglas suggested we return to the house to check if our wives were suffering from the after effects of their nasty shock. Still undecided on the best course of action, I meekly followed my brother indoors where we discovered our wives in the kitchen cooing over Anastasia, the baby having woken from her nap.

With Apollo bundled out of sight, Marigold appeared to have made a remarkable recovery, she and Elaine conveniently ignoring the elephant in the room as they rifled through glossy carrier bags as though nothing at all untoward had occurred.

"I managed to get a suitable hat for your mother to wear to the christening," Marigold chirped. "Don't worry, Victor. I didn't splash out a fortune on it in Marks and Spencer. We found this little shop tucked away in a back street, not the sort of place I'd usually go in, full of dowdy clothes for older women, but we spotted this hat in the window and thought of your mother. Ah, here it is."

With a dramatic flourish Marigold produced what at first glance appeared to be a fruit basket. On closer observation I realised it was actually a wide brimmed straw hat, the brim weighed down with such an assortment of plastic fruit that it would transform my mother into a walking fruit salad.

"I know it's a bit out there and in your face, but the brim will protect Violet from the sun," Marigold said, squinting dubiously at the fruity festooned headgear as though having second thoughts.

"But will it protect her from all the wasps that she will undoubtedly attract if she swans around in that monstrosity?" I snorted. Whilst admittedly my mother had shown a liking for dangling cherries, I wasn't sure how she would react to balancing an assortment of lurid plastic apples, pears, kiwis, figs and pomegranates on her head.

"I did worry that the banana on top of the pineapple was going a bit overboard," Elaine observed. "But Marigold did say your mother isn't exactly a shrinking violet."

"Indeed, that's one thing no one could ever accuse Violet Burke of being," I admitted, musing that not being backwards about coming forwards did not necessarily equate to a willingness to make an exhibition of oneself by bedecking one's head in an overabundance of garish imitation fruit.

"Douglas, what on earth has happened to you?" Elaine asked in alarm, finally noticing that her husband was covered in angry red scratches and sticking plasters.

"Just a bit of a disagreement with the cat," Douglas said without elaborating. Although I had bathed his wounds in neat TCP and stuck on the sticking plasters, my sympathy ended there. Anyone with half a brain would surely have released that holding a squirming cat under a running tap was bound to end badly.

"Oh goodness, one wouldn't expect to see such damage inflicted by tame domestics. Victor, I do hope that you kept the twins safely away from your aggressive cats," Elaine said sniffily.

"Worry not, Elaine, your children remain scratch free," I assured her, thinking it was best to keep schtum about their clumsy efforts to wash the cats in our shower. It would certainly be better for me if Marigold did not discover that her precious bottle of Rive Gauche shower gel had been wasted on the cats and was now almost empty. I was sure to end up saddled with the blame.

"So what did you all get up to today?"

Marigold asked, biting her tongue rather than reacting to Elaine maligning the good name of her cats.

"Well, taking care of two children and two babies certainly kept us busy," I replied.

"Two babies? Victor, have you been drinking?" Marigold accused, firing a withering look in my direction.

"Dina left little Nikoleta with me for the day, she had some sort of emergency. Perish the thought that I would indulge in alcohol whilst in charge of tender infants," I protested.

"Uncle Bucket, can you get *ouzo* and *raki* for us," Millie and Tilly shouted, running into the kitchen. Intercepting the withering look that Elaine fired in my direction, I surmised that I had gone down in her estimation, clearly relegated to the role of the disreputable alcoholic uncle plying her underage children with fiery Greek spirits.

"We don't allow the chickens in the house," Marigold said to the girls.

"Chickens?" Elaine parroted.

"Yes, oh surely you didn't think that Victor…" Marigold defended.

"Really, Elaine, get a grip. Raki and Ouzo are part of Victor's brood," Douglas impatiently interrupted. "I keep telling you that Vic is nothing like Terry."

"Victor," I corrected.

"Can we have ice cream, please, please, Uncle Bucket," the twins begged in unison.

"Certainly not…" I said.

"Victor, don't be such a spoil sport, they are on holiday after all," Marigold scolded.

"But they very conveniently neglected to mention that we have already taken them out for ice cream, if they have any more they will likely vomit all over the Punto on the drive back to the coast. It's bad enough that I still need to wash all trace of dead…"

"Victor, not another word," Marigold warned before I could tactlessly blurt out the word dog.

"We kept the children entertained by taking them out to see the local animals and then we experimented with Greek dishes for the diet plan," Douglas said.

"Mummy, can we have a pet pig, please, please?" Tilly interrupted.

"Like the one we met with the ice cream," Millie piped up.

"Dimitris introduced the girls to his pig on the way back from the shop," I explained. "He bought it with the money he won appearing on the Greek version of 'Who Wants to be a Millionaire.'

"Victor was his phone a friend," Marigold boasted, before adding, "I'm sure a nice kitten would be a much more suitable pet than a pig."

I decided not to burst my wife's innocent bubble by describing how our nieces had tormented her pampered felines; it was bound to get out about her precious Rive Gauche if I raised the matter. Instead I neatly side-stepped the issue by telling Marigold that we'd had the misfortune to run into Sherry at the shop.

"Was that the old witch?" Tilly asked.

"No, the witch was our elderly neighbour Kyria Maria, the one with the namesake tortoise. Sherry was the overly jolly lady we bumped into in the shop," I patiently explained.

"I know, I know, the lady who made you very, very cross when she said you were an escort," Millie shouted.

I didn't need to look at Elaine to sense her withering look as she jumped to the conclusion that I had a side-line as a male gigolo.

"Sherry said you were an escort, how preposterous. Had she been drinking?" Marigold sneered.

"For some bizarre reason she insisted on contradicting me when I referred to myself as a rep, pedantically arguing that as I am paid to escort people around then technically I am an escort," I said. "Personally I think it sounds utterly pretentious to label myself as an escort rather than the more recognisable rep or tour guide."

"How utterly ridiculous of Sherry, if you go around calling yourself an escort people will get completely the wrong idea. Imagine the gossip; I can just hear it now, a bunch of curtain-twitchers speculating, 'Do you think Marigold knows what her husband is up to behind her back?' Really such unfortunate terminology would make me a laughing stock," Marigold scoffed.

Elaine's reaction rather proved the point that the use of the term escort would only result in smutty thoughts and sniggering from a bunch of nosey-parkers with too much idle time on their hands. "The sooner we fix Sherry up with a man the sooner she is likely to forget all about escorts."

"Don't drag me into it, I'm having nothing to do with your interfering matchmaking," I said firmly. The less I knew about Marigold's plans to attempt to pair Sherry off with one of the local pensioners at Apostolos' name day party, the better.

"I was really surprised that after being introduced to Sherry in the shop she immediately started badgering Vic about how to go about getting a job with him. I had her pegged as a bossy schoolmarm," Douglas interjected, provoking Marigold's eyebrows to rise in a questioning fashion.

"Sherry has decided that since none of the village ex-pats seemed too interested in joining one of her jolly clubs that she could perhaps occupy her time by repping," I explained.

"I think you mean escorting," Douglas laughed.

"The woman freely admitted she's never had a job in her life, yet she had the audacity to presume there was no particular skill to what I do," I huffed.

"Well, you were the one that suggested she find a job," Marigold reminded me.

"It wasn't meant as an invitation to encroach on my territory," I said. "Can you imagine Sherry guiding a group of tourists? She would be a total nightmare, endlessly blowing the company whistle to chivvy them along. Not every day tripper would willingly put up with such forced jollity. The idea is a joke. Sherry clearly doesn't understand how much preparation is involved; one must do hours of research to be properly familiar with the area and local customs, and at least a smattering of Greek is pretty essential too."

"Well, not everyone has your high standards, dear. Remember that rather lumpy girl with the dreadful hair? I seem to recall you complaining she was terribly bossy and inept, and couldn't speak Greek," Marigold said.

"You're like thinking of Tiffany, like," I reminded her, chortling to myself as I recalled my role in having the orange blob sent back to England. "She was like a total nightmare, much too young and inexperienced to like deal with discerning travellers. She would have been better suited to one of those dreadful 18 to 30 like resorts."

"I'd forgotten how she indiscrimately dropped the word like into every sentence," Marigold chuckled. I bit my tongue as I smiled at my wife; it wouldn't do to mention that Tiffany's habit of overusing the word like reminded me of Marigold's enthusiasm for superfluous exclamation marks.

"Anyone home?" Barry called from the door, bounding straight in. Sweeping up his baby daughter, he smothered her in sloppy kisses, Anastasia rewarding him with a delighted gurgle.

Since this was Barry's first time meeting my newly discovered half-brother and his family, Marigold made introductions all round.

"I can definitely see a bit of a resemblance," Barry said, peering intently from Douglas to me. "I really appreciate you taking Anastasia for the day. Thank goodness we're almost finished working at Sherry's place; she's worn Vangelis' patience really thin. I swear he'll swing for her if she stubs one more of his cigarettes out in his *frappé* or lectures him about shedding pastry crumbs when he tucks into a *tyropita*."

"Vangelis is a bit of a coffee and cheese pie addict," I explained to Douglas.

"We were just talking about Sherry, we ran into her in the village shop," Douglas volunteered.

"Oh, I know, Vangelis and I heard all about it when she got back." Barry's words were accompanied with a quite dramatic roll of the eyes. "Can you believe she was gushing about how cute your baby niece was, Victor, without the slightest clue that Anastasia is actually my daughter?"

"How strange, she must be very self-absorbed," Elaine astutely noted.

"Well, the likes of Sherry aren't really into hobnobbing with their tradesmen. In her eyes we're a bit like that nasty layer of plankton in the ecological pond, of little consequence," Barry snorted. "She certainly changed her tune when she discovered today that I'm related to you, Victor. She rather hilariously presumed I might have some influence in you landing her a job with the tour company. I didn't bother enlightening her that my wife is the office manager and has the ultimate say in who is employed."

"Just don't go putting in a good word on her behalf with Cynthia. I'd rather jack it in and go back to cheffing in the taverna than endure all that jolly-hockey-sticks gumpf all day," I warned.

"Don't worry, Victor. I'm sure that Sherry will have a new bee in her bonnet by tomorrow, she has the attention span of a gnat," Barry chuckled. "I forgot to mention, I bumped into Panos on the way over. His guard dog has escaped and he is rather desperate to find it. I don't suppose any of you lot have happened to see it?"

An awkward silence descended on the kitchen,

broken by Elaine jumping up and suggesting that the girls show her the chickens. As soon as the room was free of impressionable children, Barry noted, "The mood has suddenly gone a bit sombre in here. What's happened? Has somebody died?"

"It was an accident," Marigold cried, hysteria creeping into her voice. "I didn't mean to kill it."

Barry rushed over to put a comforting arm around his sister as the whole sorry saga came out. Barry's head swivelled between the three of us in consternation as we filled him in on the details.

"So, you're saying that you dragged Panos' dead dog into Guzim's shed in the hopes that no one will discover that Marigold murdered it. You've not exactly thought this through, have you?"

Douglas and I hung our heads in abject shame as Barry continued to point out the obvious flaws we had overlooked. "Guzim is likely to be home anytime soon. How do you intend to explain that a dead dog just happened to wander into his shed? I'm guessing that it closed the door behind itself."

Douglas and I shared a look of panicked

alarm as the sound of an engine idling outside on the street drifted upwards. "In fact isn't that Guzim home on his moped now?" Barry asked.

Sidling over to the balcony I surreptitiously peered down, stuttering, "No, it's much worse, it's Panos' tractor."

Chapter 8

Risen from the Dead

An ominous silence prevailed in the kitchen as we listened in frozen horror to the sound of Panos' wellies stomping up the outside stairs. I could only presume that the guilt written all over Marigold and Douglas' faces was reflected in my own. Shrugging his shoulders and sending one of Marigold's withering looks in our direction, Barry shuffled over to the door to greet Panos. Despite her guilt, Marigold still had the nerve to wince when Barry invited the local farmer to step into the kitchen without first insisting he remove his mud smeared boots.

Dispensing with the usual polite formalities, Panos got straight down to business, asking if we had seen his dog.

"Echeis dei to skyli mou?"

"O skylos sou," I parroted, my deliberately blank expression attempting to convey the impression that Panos owning a dog was news to me.

"Nai, to sykli mou. To eides simera to proi." Panos' reminder that I had seen his dog only that morning left me a tad tongue-tied, only able to blurt out, *"Ach, afto to skyli."* In translation my bumbling reply means, "Ah, that dog!" and fully deserves the addition of one of Marigold's cherished exclamation marks, or *to thavmastiko* as the much overused form of punctuation is known in Greek.

"Koitaxe to schoini tou kai drapetefse, echo koitaxe pantou." Panos explained that his dog had bitten through the rope and escaped, and he had been looking for it everywhere. Unable to look Panos in the eye, Marigold's head swivelled frantically as she looked desperately round the kitchen as though the elusive hound

might have slipped in under her nose without her noticing. Before any of us could come up with any remotely plausible porky, Panos continued, declaiming that he should have known that the wart-faced old hag in the shop was a poisonous tattletale who couldn't be trusted.

"Pos kai etsi?" I said, a tad confused as to how Despina had suddenly taken centre stage in Panos' rant. "How so?"

Walking back over to the doorway and gesticulating down to the garden, Panos shouted that the malicious mother of the shopkeeper had given him an expletive laden mouthful about Apollo rampaging wildly through the village like Cerberus. At this point Barry interrupted for clarification since the analogy of Apollo to the multi-headed dog that guarded Hades had gone completely over his head.

Once Barry was brought up to speed on Greek mythology, Panos continued his tale, saying that Despina had told him she had been tempted to take a shotgun to his beloved dog until that stupid English woman had hit the creature with her car and saved her the bother of searching for ammunition. At least I think that was the gist of Panos' diatribe before he announced that it was all a pack of lies and

Despina needed certifying.

"Pos tha borouse i Despina na pei oti o sklyos mou itan nekros otan ekei diatrechei ton kipo sas, koita?" Panos roared, asking me how Despina could say that his dog was dead when there it was running through my garden.

Marigold and I were united in bewilderment as we joined Panos at the door, completely shocked to see the apparently dead Apollo tearing across our garden in heated pursuit of Guzim. The Albanian shed dweller unleashed a guttural scream of anguish as the ferocious guard dog sank its glistening fangs into his bottom, leaving a patch of bare skin exposed as it slobbered all over the torn pieces of cloth now stuck in its teeth. It seemed that the dog had managed to not only snaffle a sizeable piece of material from the seat of Guzim's trousers, but a chunk of his grubby underpants too. Before the dog could inflict any more damage on Guzim, Panos whistled sharply and called it off. At the sound of its master's voice the dog playfully rolled on its back, transformed into a picture of innocence waiting to have its tummy tickled.

"But I thought it was dead..." Marigold gasped, instinctively clapping a hand over her mouth when she realised what she had blurted out, before remembering that Panos does not understand a word of English.

"What on earth?" Douglas was clearly flabbergasted, at a complete loss as to what was going on since he had been unable to make head or tail of our Greek conversation. I felt equally bewildered, baffled how the dog had miraculously managed to rise from the dead. It was certainly unfortunate that we hadn't heard Guzim return or we would have waylaid him with some feeble excuse about why he shouldn't go into his shed until we'd managed to bury the dog. It struck me that the latter point was now moot; there would be no need to surreptitiously shovel a hole by moonlight since there was no longer a disgusting canine corpse to dispose of.

Pulling a dog collar and lead from his pocket, Panos wasted no time in heading down to the garden to reunite with his vile mutt. The sight of the dog slobbering all over its master, leaving a visible trail of drool, caused my stomach to somersault in disgust.

"I really don't understand…I was sure that I'd killed it," Marigold cried.

"I told you we should have given it the kiss of life," Douglas said.

"Seeing that it was never actually dead, that may have been a tad superfluous," I said. "Anyway, since it wasn't dead it could well have had your nose off if you'd tried the kiss of life."

"We should have checked if it had a pulse," Douglas pointed out.

"Well, hindsight is a wonderful thing," I replied, thinking there was really no point in labouring the issue; it would be like flogging a dead dog. Clearly we had jumped to the erroneous conclusion that Marigold had killed the creature, never once considering it had only been temporarily knocked out by its unfortunate collision with the car.

Guzim's dramatic cries of pain pricked my conscience and I considered that he was either milking the situation for all it was worth or that he had suffered a genuine injury. Realising that by dumping the seemingly dead dog in Guzim's shed, I was in fact directly responsible for the state he was in, I belatedly hurried down to the garden once Panos had secured Apollo to the washing line pole.

"Ponaei, ponaei." Guzim's pitiful cries that it hurt seemed a tad unnecessary since the words were expelled between shrieks of self-explanatory pain. Whilst not wishing to get any closer

to my gardener's exposed posterior than necessary, I couldn't fail to notice that Apollo had left his teeth marks in Guzim's flesh. I shuddered involuntarily at the sight; it certainly looked painful and would most definitely require a tetanus shot if Guzim was not up to date with his vaccinations.

"*Eichate ena plano tetanou*?" I said, asking him if he'd had a tetanus shot.

"*Ti*?" His reply of "what" led me to surmise he was not up to date and thus at risk of contracting the hideous jaw-locking disease from the dog bite.

"*Ti yinetai me ti lyssa*?" I added, the sight of the slobbering dog making me worry if Guzim was at risk from rabies.

"*O skylos mou den echei lyssa,*" Panos shouted, adamantly declaring that his dog did not have rabies.

"*Guzim, chreiazeste rammata kai ena tetano. Ela, prepei na pame stin klinki.*" My advice that we must go to the clinic as Guzim needed stitches and a tetanus shot was met by an almost indecipherable torrent of Greek peppered with what I presumed were Albanian expletives.

"*Mila arga.*" In my most commanding tone, I instructed Guzim to speak slowly. Taking a deep breath, Guzim complained between squeals of pain that he couldn't go to the clinic as he had no insurance. Furthermore he had no cash to pay for the treatment because his wife in Albania had eaten all his money. Fortunately I was able to readily translate since the latter point was one of Guzim's frequent laments that I was all too familiar with.

Since I felt directly responsible for Guzim's condition, I did not hesitate to assure him that I would pay for whatever treatment was required. Before I had finished voicing my undoubtedly generous offer, Panos interrupted to insist that he would pay for the treatment since it was his dog that had taken a bite out of Guzim's bottom. Whilst Panos and I argued over which of us would foot the bill, Guzim went off on a tangent, insisting that he couldn't possibly go to the clinic with his bottom on display, bellyaching that his best trousers were ruined.

Fortunately, I was able to come up with a fortuitous solution to his latest complaint: heading over to Guzim's shed I retrieved the trousers that Maria had discarded that morning which we had used to drag the dog. Holding the trousers at arm's length in case they were flea infested from their contact with Apollo, I chucked them at Guzim, telling him to put them on so that we could head off to the clinic.

Holding the trousers up for critical inspection, Guzim whined that they were horrible, *"Afta ta pantelonia einai frikta."* I sighed in exasperation; now really wasn't the time for the Albanian shed dweller to belatedly develop a sense of style.

"Einai dorean." "They are free", I snapped, adding in what I am sure was most ungrammatical Greek that if they were good enough for Papas Andreas they were certainly good enough for a snivelling wretch like him.

Since Panos and I were each ridden with guilt over Guzim's nasty wound, it was decided we would both accompany him to the clinic on the coast. After consulting with Marigold, it was arranged that she would drive Douglas and his family back to the coast where we would meet up for dinner later once Guzim was stitched up, leaving me no choice but to head down there in the tractor. I supposed that was convenient as it would allow Panos and me to continue our squabble over who would pay for Guzim's medical expenses during the drive.

Whilst I was less than enthusiastic about the

prospect of the bone shaking journey down in the tractor, at least the arrangement meant that Guzim wouldn't be bleeding all over the Punto.

Chapter 9

Stinking of Ouzo

Guzim and I exchanged horrified looks when we learnt that Panos intended to drag his ferocious guard dog along with us to the medical centre on the coast. With the anguish of temporarily losing his beloved mutt still ripe in his mind, the welly wearing farmer flatly refused to be parted from the brute again. At least we were spared from enduring the beast riding with us in the close confines of the cab. Instead, Panos tied it up inside the tractor trailer he refused to uncouple, despite the obvious slowing us down implications of towing the trailer through a succession of hairpin bends.

Since it seemed advisable for Guzim to avoid sitting on his suppurating wound until he had received medical treatment, he ended up sprawled facedown across my legs; the tractor cab being a tad on the small size, making it a bit of a squeeze. I would hazard a guess that Panos' tractor is of the same vintage as its owner. Whilst Panos keeps a superficially clean but untidy house, the ancient tractor cab is best described as a dustbin on wheels, chock full of discarded *ION* chocolate wrappers, muddy farm implements and a bucket of rancid smelling chicken feed.

There was even a manky old bone displaying evidence of a good gnawing, tossed aside in the footwell. The detritus of dog hairs hinted that Apollo was more used to travelling up front with its owner than being relegated to the trailer, a suspicion soon confirmed when due to unwanted proximity, I was able to compare the teeth marks on the bone to those on Guzim's bottom. Unfortunately, the bottom in question was almost fully exposed because Papas Andreas' trousers refused to stay up, being far too baggy for their scrawny beneficiary. With little else to occupy my attention, I became a tad too familiar with Guzim's buttocks during the tiresome, bone jolting ride.

With my legs pinned down by Guzim's weight, the journey was off to an excruciatingly uncomfortable start. Attempting to shake a leg to avoid pins and needles setting in, my foot encountered a fetid takeout bag from Goody's Burger House, the popular Greek fast food chain. My mind boggled; since the nearest branch is located on the seafront in town, I wondered if Panos had actually made the long journey for take-out by tractor. We were barely out of Meli but our juddering crawl of a pace meant that we were already creating an endless traffic jam, angry drivers hooting their horns behind us, unable to overtake on the bends due to the addition of Panos' trailer swinging erratically across the central white line. The line of drivers was forced to suffer the suffocating smoky emissions belched out from the tractor's rather ropey exhaust, held in place with the silver duct-tape more usually associated with patching up *somba* pipes. I considered that if Panos had insisted on driving the tractor all the way to town in search of greasy fast food, it would surely represent an open invitation for a fellow road user to succumb to justifiable road rage.

Doubtful that the tractor was even hitting the dizzy speed of fifteen kilometres an hour, I pondered it may well have been quicker to telephone Poppy's father and ask him to pop up to Meli and stitch the Albanian's bottom together. With Guzim's low standards, I doubted he would feel any personal shame in being sewn up by a veterinarian. The noise of the engine was deafening, the vibrations adding to the discomfort I was suffering from the unshakeable pins and needles. I couldn't even drown the noise out by singing along to the latest Eurovision chart topper on the radio, since the tractor lacked such a modern amenity. How I longed to belt out the chorus of 'Die for You' simply to relieve the interminable howls of pain Guzim emitted at regular intervals. Whilst not wishing to malign his character, I rather suspected he was milking his injury for all it was worth.

Panos nudged me sharply in the ribs, bellowing something that was hard to decipher against the competing noise of Guzim's groaning and the din of the engine. Catching the words *"Ena boukali ouzo,"* and following Panos' gesture, I concluded that he had a bottle of *ouzo* stashed away under the seat.

"Ochi efcharisto." I politely declined his offer of a drink.

"Ochi yia sena, dose ston Guzim yia ton pono," Panos yelled, recklessly removing his eyes from the road and rolling them at me. In truth the very expressive eye roll made me a tad ashamed that Panos had needed to point out that I should give the *ouzo* to Guzim to help with the pain.

"Malista." Pushing Guzim's prostrate body to one side, I groped around under the seat for the bottle. My clumsy attempt to pour the strong smelling spirit down Guzim's gullet, no easy task considering his prone position across my knee, resulted in half the contents of the bottled soaking into Papas Andreas' cast-off trousers. I mused that perhaps the spillage over Guzim's exposed buttock may well numb his open wound. It was a stroke of bad luck that my inexact aim would likely label the Albanian shed dweller a raging alcoholic when we reached our destination.

Rounding a corner, Panos slammed on the brakes as the tractor met the inevitable procession of goats tripping across the road. Cutting the engine while we waited for the goats to disperse allowed us to hear one another clearly for the first time since we had climbed in the cab. I complained to Panos that it was taking an absolute age to crawl to the clinic and expressed my hope that we wouldn't be kept waiting endlessly on our arrival. Panos put my mind at ease by assuring me that most people found it more convenient to be sick in the mornings and at this time of day the clinic was sure to be empty.

Guzim demanded to know how Panos' fearsome dog had managed to get inside his shed. Panos, still oblivious to the truth, told Guzim that he must be confused, but the toothless Albanian retorted that he had suffered a vicious bite to the bottom, not a confusion inducing bump on the head. Guzim was adamant that he knew what he saw: the dog had been lying in wait to attack him the moment he opened the door to the shed. Panos wasted no time in attempting to get to the bottom of things, suggesting that Guzim must have left the door open and the dog had wandered innocently inside.

Guzim emphatically denied it, insisting he had shut the door firmly when he went off to work so that Doruntina couldn't escape. He made no attempt to mince his words when he shouted that he didn't trust the old witch next door not to cook his pet rabbit if she managed to get her hands on it. I reflected that Guzim may have a valid point as I certainly recall Kyria Maria mentioning she was quite partial to a nice dish of stewed rabbit flavoured with a sprig of fresh rosemary.

"Den mageirevei ti helona," I said, pointing out in Maria's defence that she hadn't cooked the tortoise that she'd found in her garden.

Fortunately, the last of the goats skipped into the olive groves before Panos had chance to delve any deeper into the mystery of how his dog ended up in the shed. The noise of the engine once again drowned out any further attempts at conversation, thus keeping my dirty little secret safe a while longer. All I had to do was maintain my cool and Panos would remain none the wiser that I had fully intended to cover up my wife's collision with his dog by first concealing, and then burying, the evidence.

Finally parked up at the clinic after the torturous journey, we helped the injured Guzim down from the cab, Panos and I still squabbling in a friendly manner about which one of us would pick up his medical tab. Considering the dog would likely never have attacked Guzim if I hadn't dumped it in his shed, I felt a moral obligation to be the one to cover the costs of Guzim's treatment, Panos feeling the same sense of duty since he had been at fault by failing to keep Apollo securely chained.

Leaving me to support the *ouzo* stinking Guzim, the farmer swanned off to the trailer to give the dog water.

"Ela, ti einai afto, o skylos echei molopes," Panos shouted in consternation. My translation skills were not up to the job. Although I knew that Panos had said, "What is this, the dog has…" what the dog had remained a mystery since *molopes* was beyond the scope of my memorised Greek vocabulary. From the expression on Panos' face, I surmised that whatever it was, it wasn't good.

"Mia megali molopa," Panos repeated, furrowing his brow as he searched for an alternative word to convey his meaning. *"Melania."* The penny dropped; Panos was telling me that the dog had a bruise.

"Eisai sigouros?" I feebly enquired if he was sure, my heart hammering in my chest as he surveyed the extent of the canine damage.

"Nai, eimai sigouros, ela kai koita." My heart sank as Panos confirmed he was sure, waving me over to come and look. *"Pos to katalave?"* As

Panos queried how the dog got the bruise, I felt my face redden, my blushing complexion reflecting my guilt.

"Victor, xereis kati, pes mou." I squirmed as Panos stared me down, saying I must tell him if I knew something. Looking at the ground, I shuffled my feet, evading his question by muttering that we really needed to get Guzim inside for medical attention. Panos, clearly sensing that something was amiss, started shouting that perhaps Despina was not quite as mad as he'd thought; perhaps she really had witnessed a car hitting his dog.

In order to do full justice to the ensuing exchange of dialogue, I will simply pen Panos' words in English so that any readers that have stuck with the story, even after despairing of my assumed complicity in canicide, may better appreciate the flow of conversation. It certainly didn't flow as clearly as scripted, peppered with numerous language faux pas and cries of *"ti"* as we struggled to understand one another. Heated Greek can prove a tad difficult to decipher.

"The old bag swore blind that a stupid English woman drove into my dog," Panos shouted.

"That wart-faced old hag has a nerve calling

my wife stupid," I blurted. "Marigold is anything but stupid. She has a degree in food science, you know."

"No, I didn't know that, I thought she had you under the thumb doing most of the cooking…hang on, do you mean to tell me that Despina really did see Marigold drive into my dog?"

"Well, not strictly speaking. Your dog ran into the Punto, in fact according to Marigold it positively hurled itself in her path, frothing at the mouth it was too," I said. Whilst Marigold hadn't specifically referred to any frothing, I thought it was a salient touch to add, if a tad hyperbolic. "It's a good job that Marigold and Elaine both had their seat belts fastened securely or they may have suffered an injury."

"So your car hit my dog…hang on, how did it get in Guzim's shed?"

"I confess that I did have a hand in putting the dog in the shed…we thought it best if the children didn't see the dog in that state in case it upset them."

"What state? Hang on, you mean to say that you knew that the dog was injured and yet you went ahead and dumped it in the shed?" Panos practically spat.

"Well, not exactly. We didn't realise the dog was injured..."

"That's a relief," Panos interrupted.

"We thought it was dead," I continued, cringing as I blurted this little gem out.

"You thought Apollo was dead..."

"But I thought it best to get it out of the heat, I know from experience how nasty sunstroke can be," I improvised, hoping to play on Panos' sympathy if he'd heard about my recent malady.

"You blithering moron, dead dogs don't get sunstroke," Panos bellowed, balling his fists in anger. Taking a step backwards in case the farmer had some ridiculous notion of thumping me, I knocked into Guzim who was holding onto the tractor for support.

"Voithise me, chreiazomai yiatro," Guzim cried out, whining for help and saying he needed a doctor.

Using Guzim as a convenient excuse, I slung his arm over my shoulder, telling Panos I needed to get the Albanian inside the clinic.

"Po-po, den peirazei ton Alvano, ti yinetai me to skyli mou," Panos yelled, pushing past me to barge into the clinic first. I found it a tad callous that Panos told me to never mind about the

Albanian, what about his dog; then again he has never had much liking for my toothless gardener. Even so, there was certainly no need for him to allow the glass door to slam in our faces. It was a terribly ill-mannered gesture.

Ignoring Guzim's exaggerated cries of pain, the receptionist told us to take a seat, obviously a difficult feat in Guzim's case considering the rather delicate position of his injury. Panos demonstrated that he had no intention of being fobbed off, banging his fist on the counter and demanding that a doctor be sent out to his trailer immediately to tend to a gravely injured patient. Even though Panos rattled through his demands at great speed, it didn't escape my notice that he failed to identify the injured patient as canine.

A white coated youngster, still too wet behind the ears to have started shaving, emerged from an examination room, demanding to know what all the shouting was about. Presuming the fellow must be a trainee doctor, I mused that medical professionals must be following the course charted by the proverbial policemen, getting ever younger.

"Ela exo yiatro, o asthenis einai sto trailer mou,"

Panos pleaded, grabbing the doctor's sleeve and telling him to come outside, the patient was in his trailer.

"Einai mono enas skylos, o Guzim ponaei," I interrupted, letting the doctor know that the patient was only a dog and that Guzim was in pain. To my mind it was self-evident that Guzim, an actual human, should take precedence with the doctor over a dog.

"Ena aftokinito chtypise ton skylo," Panos shouted, telling the doctor that a car had hit the dog.

"Alla o skylos den travmatistike otan epitethike Guzim," I said, pointing out that the dog wasn't hurt when it attacked Guzim.

Clucking his tongue, Panos threw his head back in a contemptuous gesture of disbelief before sending a litany of rapid fire Greek in my direction. I struggled to make sense of Panos' words, but once I had mentally translated them I realised he had won the argument. I had to admit that I couldn't argue with his point that I'd thought the dog was dead and one couldn't get more hurt than dead.

For some inexplicable reason, the doctor assumed that I was British and addressed me directly in English. Nodding towards Guzim, he wrinkled his nose in distaste, saying, "The drunk will have to the wait, this man has an injured dog."

Before I could protest that Guzim was perfectly sober and I was responsible for his clothing being soaked with ouzo, the doctor had rushed outside with Panos. As they exited the clinic, I could hear the doctor telling the farmer he was a great dog lover and had a *kokoni* of his own, Panos responding that it was a lovely breed.

I could hardly believe my ears when the doctor called for a stretcher to be sent outside to the trailer. I reflected that the filthy mutt had been chasing after Guzim at speed only an hour earlier and was perfectly capable of using its legs. Nevertheless the dog was stretchered into the clinic and wheeled straight into the examination room the doctor had previously emerged from, displacing an old and frail looking Greek granny who had been mid-examination before the rumpus.

Apparently unconcerned that she had been turfed out mid-way through her consultation to make room for a dog, the elderly woman sat down next to me in the waiting area. Fingering a couple of stray hairs sprouting from her chin, she confided that she hoped that the dog would be okay, *"Elpizo oti i skylos tha einai entaxei."*

Staring at Guzim with disdain, she wrinkled her nose in abject revulsion. Leaning in close to me, she whispered, *"Oti ta alvanika myrizei ouzo, einai aidiastiko."* I don't think that Guzim overheard her saying that it was disgusting the way the Albanian stunk of ouzo; he was too busy putting on a dramatic show for the benefit of the receptionist, moaning loudly whilst conducting a running battle to keep Papas Andreas' shabby old trousers from falling down. It was really too bad that Kyria Maria had not added a convenient belt to our bartering bucket.

Since Guzim had only groaned rather than spoken, I was curious how the old lady knew that he was Albanian; his distinctive guttural accent was the usual giveaway that he hailed from the impoverished East European nation. Since it had always intrigued me how Greeks could spot an Albanian at twenty paces, I asked the old woman how she could pinpoint his country of origin simply by looking at him.

"Einai to epipedo kefali," she hissed. I immediately stared at Guzim to determine if it was true that he had a flat head. It wasn't something

that had registered with me until that moment as a national trait.

After an interminable wait, Panos and Apollo came out of the examination room, the doctor petting the dog as though it was an adorable puppy rather than a trained-to-kill guard dog. Whilst Panos led his dog back to the trailer, the doctor came over and instructed Guzim to show him his injury, a simple act that only required the Albanian to surrender his hold on the waistband of Papas Andreas' trousers in order to flash his dog bitten bottom. Ushering the elderly woman back into the examination room before the sight of naked flesh could provoke an attack of the vapours, the medic ignored Guzim and spoke directly to me. Telling me that he would stitch the wound shortly, he asked if I would like to come in with Guzim to watch him in action and admire his recently acquired skill with the needle. I politely declined, having seen quite enough of Guzim's bottom to last me a lifetime.

Appearing a tad deflated that my lack of interest in his needlework would deprive him of an admiring audience, the young doctor suggested I should pop down to the local pharmacy to buy the dose of Tenivac required for the administration of the tetanus shot. Since the doctor had insisted on addressing me in English, Guzim remained clueless to what was going on. Patting his arm, I told him I was off to the pharmacy to buy the necessary ingredients for his tetanus jab and that I would return to settle any expenses he incurred for his treatment.

"Victor, alla fovamai tis velones," Guzim stuttered, telling me he was frightened of needles.

"Tha einai entaxei, mono ena mikro tsimpima." For some reason Guzim appeared to draw little comfort when I told him that it would be okay, just one little prick. By the time I escaped Guzim's clutches he was practically a gibbering wreck, his nerves so badly frayed that it wouldn't surprise me if he attempted to suck the last drop of spilt *ouzo* out of Papas Andreas' trousers.

Chapter 10

A Plate of Shared Sardines

I was rather taken aback by the instruction to purchase the necessary ingredient for the tetanus shot from the pharmacy. In my admittedly limited experience with the National Health Service back in Manchester, I could not recall being sent out to buy any injectable liquids necessary for vaccinations, only ever being asked to proffer my arm or my bottom before receiving a jab when holidaying in countries where travel vaccines were a requirement. Once again, I was learning something new about the Greek way of doing things.

The smell of freshly cut grass pervaded the air outside the clinic, a welcome respite from the overpowering combination of *ouzo* and disinfectant inside. Panos was leaning against his tractor, the smoke from the cigarette he was puffing away on polluting the humid air. I felt a stab of shame at the way I had so readily deceived Panos, prioritising protecting my own hide over his feelings for his beloved dog. Keeping my distance in case the farmer was still inclined to thump me, I was taken aback to say the least when Panos strode over, throwing a friendly arm across my shoulder and asking where I was going, *"Ela Victor, pou pas kale file mou?"*

It was a huge weight off my mind to hear Panos address me as his good friend. It was clear he was no longer inclined to give me a good thrashing, a great relief since I abhor any displays of violence, particularly if there is the remotest chance I will be on the receiving end. I attribute this to a hangover from the childhood torment I had suffered at the grubby hands of Derek Little. After I explained that I needed to go the pharmacy to buy the necessary for Guzim's shot, Panos told me there was a good half hour to kill until the pharmacy opened, if the pharmacist could even be bothered to open on time, which was very doubtful in his opinion. It seemed that the place operated on Greek time.

"Ela file mou, pame yia kafe." Recalling that not half an hour earlier, Panos had been on the verge of thumping me, I readily accepted the generous invitation to join him for coffee, hoping the olive branch he offered represented a chance to bury the hatchet, rather than some cynical trick. I must confess to a slight feeling of trepidation when Panos put Apollo on the lead, but the dog appeared to be relatively docile, at least in comparison to when it had been sinking its teeth into Guzim.

The dog took the lead as we made the short stroll to the nearest *kafenion,* a rather quaint harbourside establishment frequented by the local fishermen. We claimed two rather uncomfortable hard backed chairs directly overlooking the sea, Apollo settling down under the table at his master's feet. A couple of cats that had been lazing in the sunshine took one look at the dog and scarpered pretty sharpish, adopting a new spot next to a ceramic pot of cheerful red geraniums on the harbour wall. There was something about the *kafenion* that reminded me of Nikos' taverna. It had the same spit and sawdust, no frills approach, offering little more than the basics of *Ellinikos kafe, ouzo* and *tavli. Souvlaki* was on offer for hungry regulars and for the odd tourist brave enough to venture into a place they were sure to be stared at and that lacked the frills of more comfortable establishments.

A couple of local fishermen exchanged greetings with Panos, whilst casting curious glances in my direction, reminding me of the way the taverna regulars warily check out any new arrivals they are unfamiliar with. The fishermen continued to give me the silent once-over until they heard me place my order for coffee in Greek, at which point they grunted approvingly before returning their attention to their game of *tavli*.

Panos quizzed the *kafenion* owner, a tall balding chap with a prominent gut straining against the confines of his shirt, about the freshness of the sardines. Once assured they were barely off the boat and out of the nets, Panos ordered a plate of *tiganites sardeles* to accompany our coffee. Accustomed to the local practice of sharing a plate of food for the table, I looked forward to snacking on the fried sardines, hoping they would put an end to the embarrassing noises emanating from my rumbling stomach: the *maroulosalata* I had enjoyed for lunch could not exactly be described as filling. As my stomach emitted another unsociable growl of hunger, I made a point of firing one of Marigold's withering looks at the dog, hoping to distract attention from my involuntary rumblings by shifting the blame.

We waited in companionable silence for our coffees, I for one feeling relieved that our friendship was restored and that the awkward business with the dog had apparently not done any lasting damage to our mutual camaraderie. Panos had been one of the first villagers to extend the hand of friendship to me when I had first settled in Meli, plying me with a carrier bag of plump grapes freshly plucked from his vine. Communication between us could be a bit hit and miss, but I was always guaranteed a warm welcome at his table if I popped in to the taverna for a drink. He was always my first port of call when I needed advice about the health of the chickens or the growth spurt of my vegetables.

I felt the warmth of the sun relaxing the tension in my shoulders as I gazed out to sea, appreciating the tranquil beauty of the view.

Barely a ripple disturbed the almost glass-like surface of the clear blue water, picturesquely dotted with moored fishing boats. In the distance a small boat changed course to head back to shore. As it grew closer I began to discern the deep blue stripe encircling the wooden vessel and a rather incongruous plastic chair positioned beneath a faded flimsy canopy that may once have been white. The fisherman skilfully steered the boat towards its mooring, attracting the attention of a number of English tourists strolling past the *kafenion*. They stopped to watch the boat's progress with interest, the melodic putter of the engine competing with their excited chatter as background noise. The tourists continued on their way once the fisherman cut the engine, tethering the boat by lassoing a rope to a harbour post.

"Yassou Thoma, kalo piasimo?" the fishermen at the adjacent table yelled out, asking the fisherman if he had a good catch. As he turned to answer, I recognised the boatman as the chap who delivers fish in Meli twice a week. Marigold often makes purchases from him during the summer months. Panos called over, telling him to stop by the house with some *soupia* next time he was in Meli. I chuckled to myself,

finding it quite amusing to listen to Panos barter for fish, *"Tha sas pliroso se nektarinia yia tis soupies, fresko apo to dentro,"* promising to pay Thomas for the cuttlefish with a bag of fresh nectarines straight from the tree.

"Ftiachno kali soupa apo ti soupa," Panos said, telling me he made good soup out of cuttlefish. I smiled agreeably, thinking the charming alliteration of *soupia soupa* did not translate well into English.

The *kafenion* owner set two tiny cups of steaming Greek coffee on the table, along with two tall glasses of water. *"Victor, thes ouzo? Den odigeis,"* Panos said, asking me if I wanted *ouzo* and reminding me that I wasn't driving. I declined the spirit, my lungs still full of the stuff after breathing in Guzim's accidentally alcoholic aroma.

The *kafenion* owner returned with a platter of freshly fried sardines. They smelled absolutely delicious. Without asking me if I preferred my sardines with a squeeze of lemon, Panos picked up the two lemon quarters, surprising me by lobbing them straight into the sea. To my absolute amazement he then picked up the plate of sardines and deposited it on the floor at our feet, declaring, *"O Apollon agapa tis sardeles, alla den tou aresei to lemoni,"* informing me that Apollo loves sardines, but does not like lemon. I reflected that whatever the preferences the dog may have, there was no need to waste a full platter of the tempting fish on the beast.

Noticing my rather astonished expression, Panos slapped his forehead in apology, saying, "*Sygnomi,* Victor," before bending down to retrieve a couple of sardines from the plate. Wiping a strand of dog drool from the fish, he offered them to me. I declined. The idea of sharing a plate of food which the dog was slobbering over made my stomach recoil. When I expressed my surprise that dogs ate fish, Panos told me that Apollo would eat anything, it wasn't fussy. I had to chuckle when he added, "*Akomi kai oi gloutoi ton Alvanon,*" which translates as, 'Even the buttocks of Albanians.'

I sighed in relief when our conversation was interrupted by Panos' mobile ringing. Although I value Panos' friendship, it can get a tad taxing on the old brain matter to converse entirely in Greek without the luxury of slipping into one's mother tongue for a mental break. Sipping my strong Greek coffee, I tuned out whilst Panos chuntered away on his phone, amusing myself by watching the antics of the cats playing on the wall. Finishing his call, Panos announced that Spiros would be joining us in a moment. Always delighted to see Spiros, I perked up at the news.

Whilst we waited for the undertaker to join us, Panos said, *"Prepei na ertheis sto festival sardeles."* I assured him that I had every intention of attending the upcoming sardine festival; indeed Marigold had circled the date on our summer calendar.

Spiros ambled along the harbour in mafia shades and a suit, his choice of formal attire indicating that he had been out on funeral business. Calling out his order for *Ellinikos kafe* and *souvlaki,* he pulled up a chair to join us, loosening his tie and passing a carrier bag to Panos. I tuned out momentarily, unable to keep up with their fast-paced conversation, only mildly curious when Panos pulled a sturdy steel chain from the bag. Turning to me, Spiros explained, "I get the chain for the dog of the Panos from the hard-shop, it will to stop the monster from the escaping again."

"Hardware," I automatically corrected.

An ominous growl from beneath the table alerted Spiros to the presence of the aforesaid monster. Frowning, he backed up his chair, putting some distance between himself and Apollo as he resumed his conversation in Greek with Panos. Clearly Spiros was not a fan of the ferocious guard dog either.

"The Panos he tell to me you feel the bad about the Marigold hitting the dog with the car and the trying to hide it," Spiros said.

"I do, but fortunately the dog didn't suffer a serious injury, just a bruise. In fact the only one to suffer is Guzim, who is having his bottom sewn back together as we speak."

"He should be the grateful the dog went for the him and not for the rabbit he sleep with," Spiros chuckled. "But anyway, the Panos tell me you want to make the amend to him."

"Do I?" I didn't recall saying that, but then again my Greek is open to interpretation. Figuring it would be prudent to play along in the name of my valued friendship with Panos, I hastily added, "I do, of course. Want to make amends, I mean. Tell him whatever he needs."

I imagined my generous offer would amount to nothing more than Panos requesting I put in a good word for him with Violet Burke: I was pretty certain the welly wearing farmer had more than a soft spot for my mother, even perchance a romantic interest.

After consulting with Spiros, Panos leant

forward and gripped my arm, saying, *"Efcharisto Victor, na eisai avrio sto spiti mou stis 4.30."* The only reason I could imagine he was telling me to be at his house at 4.30 the next day was so that we could go to Apostolos' name day party together, but it struck me as a tad early. I thought the party didn't begin until the evening. Nevertheless I confirmed the arrangement that he wanted to meet at 4.30 the next day for the party, saying, *"Thelete na synantitheite stis 4.30 yia to parti tou Apostolou."*

Practically choking with laughter, Panos thumped my shoulder none too gently. When he managed to compose himself, he snorted, *"4.30 to proi, yia na me voithisei sta chorafia."*

I must have misheard; surely he wasn't seriously suggesting we meet before dawn. Turning to Spiros for clarification, I asked, "Did he just say he wants me to meet him at 4.30 in the morning to help in his fields?"

"Yes, to make the amend. For the dog. It is not so the bad, Victor, everyone know you like to get up from the bed at the early," Spiros said.

"What possible help can I be to Panos in his fields?" I asked with a hint of alarm in my voice. "I'm not exactly experienced in rounding up sheep in the dark."

"Not to the worry, the Panos he know you the frighten of his sheep, he not make you to go near them," Spiros assured me. His mocking tone left me in no doubt that the villagers were not about to forget the up close, late-night encounter that Marigold and I had with the recalcitrant sheep that had stalked Meli. "He need you to help to harvest the *vlita* and then to take to the market to sell."

"The *vlita*?"

"The small salad leaf, the green leaf. I not to know how to say the *vlita* in the English. The Panos has much to the harvest. I think you will to enjoy the selling it at the market and you will be the finish before the lunch."

"But there's nothing wrong with the dog," I objected, thinking the punishment of slaving away in Panos' fields was out of all proportion to my perceived crime.

"But to think, Victor, if you had to killed the dog the Panos would want to put this chain on your neck and have you to guard the yard. I think you have got off the easy, as they say."

"It was Marigold that hit the blasted dog, not me," I snapped in exasperation.

"Somehow, I not to see the Marigold picking the *vlita,* better that you to do it, yes."

"Well, I think it's a tad over the top..."

"I think the same about the collecting of the Violet Burke from the airport," Spiros said with a shrug. "*Ti na kanoume*?"

"Indeed, what can you do," I parroted, realising I couldn't argue with that.

Chapter 11

Cutting a Suave Figure

I had arranged to meet Marigold at the beach on the outskirts of the village when we were finished at the clinic. It was a huge relief to be spared the torturous trip back up to Meli in the tractor, especially considering another bout of Guzim's histrionics was practically a given. Nevertheless, I gladly accepted Panos' offer of a lift to the beach since it was still a tad too hot for walking and the coastal road was noticeably bereft of shade.

Since Panos and I were otherwise occupied drinking coffee when the doctor stitched up the wound on Guzim's buttock, we were able to avoid the worst of the Albanian's melodramatics. Once we returned to the clinic, we were forced to endure the public embarrassment of being associated with the needle-shy gardener, his screams of pain bouncing off the walls of the waiting area when the tetanus shot was finally administered. Although I had flatly refused Guzim's childish plea to accompany him into the examination room and hold his hand whilst he suffered the vaccination, I was at least able to assure him that his bottom was safe from any more messing by medics: the pharmacist had informed me that the tetanus shot would be injected into the shoulder.

Having stumped up the cash in the pharmacy, I generously conceded that Panos could pay for any expenses Guzim ran up at the clinic. Although the doctor refused to accept any payment despite the Albanian lacking insurance, Panos insisted on remunerating him with a convenient bag of fresh *nectarinia* he had stashed in the trailer. Recalling the way the farmer had bartered with Thomas for *soupia* in exchange for said fruit, I hazarded a guess that Panos must have a glut of the stuff he was desperate to get rid of before they turned mushy.

Since the doctor had proved so obliging, I hoped for his sake that Apollo hadn't slobbered all over the nectarines. I reflected it was bad enough that the filthy mutt had likely contaminated the clinic with its fleas, leaving the place in dire need of a thorough sanitising. It would take a sight more than a good going over with Vim to persuade me to hop on the stretcher after Apollo.

Hoisting Papas Andreas' too large trousers to waist level, Guzim climbed into the tractor cab, perching very gingerly on his bottom, whining and snivelling continually during the short drive to the beach. The moment Panos parked up to drop me off, he wasted no time in turfing Guzim out of the cab and relegating him to the trailer, assuring him that the fresh air would do him good. In truth it was Panos who craved fresh air, asphyxiated from the combined stench of *ouzo* and Guzim's rancid sweat. Bundling the guard dog into the tractor cab, Panos demonstrated he was not completely heartless, acknowledging it may be a tad callous to expect Guzim to ride alongside the dog that had taken a chunk out of his buttock. Feeling a pang of sympathy for the luckless Albanian, I surreptitiously passed him the now half-empty bottle of *ouzo* to help numb his pain.

Before driving away, Panos shook my hand heartily, reminding me that he was expecting me to roll up for *vlita* harvesting duty at 4.30 prompt the next morning. His reminder was a tad unnecessary: it was hardly the sort of thing that was likely to slip my mind.

Standing beneath the trees offering welcome shade at the back of the beach, I scanned the white sand in search of my wife, feeling the cooling draw of the sea. The sun highlighted a hint of turquoise in the inviting water, contrasting with the splash of white as foamy waves rolled over the pebbles forming a sentinel perimeter where the sand met the sea. Sprawled out on a sun lounger beneath a beach umbrella, Marigold cut a solitary figure surrounded by beach bags, her nose entrenched in one of her interminable moving-abroad books. I waved to Douglas, Elaine and the twins, barely discernable specks in the distance, frolicking in the sea: at least I hoped it was them. I wouldn't want to get a reputation for being a tad overfriendly with complete strangers.

"Gosh, that took an age; I've been waiting

for you to join us. I slipped your swim shorts into the beach bag if you want to change and enjoy a dip," Marigold said, tucking a stray red lock behind her ear and shading her eyes as she smiled up at me.

"It's a tad public for changing," I prevaricated, noticing a number of eagle-eyed sun worshippers peering intently in my direction. No doubt my arrival had piqued their curiosity. Having no way of knowing that I was married to the Titian haired beauty in the fetching green costume, I imagined they may well be speculating that I was trying to pick her up. I expect they had their fingers crossed for my success, since I was sure I cut a suave figure.

"There seems to be an awful lot of people staring our way."

"It's probably because they don't see many men wearing long slacks paired with a shirt and tie on the beach, dear. You really should at least take your socks off before they get clogged with sand," Marigold smirked, dashing my image of myself as a debonair type.

"I hardly think it would have been appropriate to turn up bare chested at the clinic in nothing more than a pair of budgie smugglers," I pointed out sullenly.

"Oh, how you exaggerate, Victor. You know full well that you wouldn't be caught dead in such tasteless garb. I'm sure the hideous sight of Harold in his budgies is permanently etched on your brain," Marigold laughed. "Are you going to change or just stand around sweating in those hot clothes?"

"It will be a bit of a squash trying to wriggle into my swim shorts in the Punto," I said, considering my options. I certainly had no intention of doing a Blackpool beach special, contorting myself awkwardly and stripping off under a towel in full view of a gawping audience.

"Why don't you simply use the facilities at the beach bar? The toilets aren't too bad. Well, at least the Ladies are relatively clean, goodness only knows what state the Gents are in," Marigold said with a shudder, gesticulating towards the establishment across the road from the beach. "You can order me a nice glass of white wine with some ice while you're there. I really could do with a drop of something to calm my nerves and help me get over the shock of that beastly dog throwing itself at the car. It really shook me up."

"Speaking of Apollo, Panos knows what happened," I told her.

"That his wild dog was roaming loose on the streets, menacing innocent drivers?" Marigold asked hopefully, having already absolved herself of all responsibility.

"He knows that you ran into his dog with the Punto, and that thinking it was dead we collaborated to hide the canine corpse in Guzim's shed."

Marigold at least had the grace to blush as she blustered, "But it's not dead, is it, so no harm done."

"Apart from the damage to our reputations if word of our underhand shenanigans gets out," I sighed.

"Surely Panos wouldn't deliberately malign your reputation, Victor, after all he's a friend of yours, not to mention he's quite sweet on your mother." I couldn't fail to notice that Marigold had consciously removed herself from the equation, expecting only my good name to be dragged through the mud even though she was technically the guilty party.

"Panos has agreed to drop the matter since I will be making amends by toiling in his fields tomorrow," I said.

"Must you talk in riddles, dear? Whatever are you on about? Toiling indeed."

"Panos press-ganged me into helping him to harvest a field of *vlita* before dawn tomorrow, and when we're finished with that we are going up to the market in town to flog the stuff."

"Well, I must say that sounds right up your street, dear. I know how much you enjoy traipsing round the market. You'll be in your element, holding court from a market stall to a captive audience; just think what a good opportunity it will be for improving your Greek. I'm sure you'll find the whole experience very jolly."

I stared at Marigold in disbelief. This rather forced jolly-hockey-sticks enthusiasm was most unlike my wife. I pondered the possibility that Marigold had been abducted by aliens and returned as a cloned personality of Sherry.

"I'm not sure I'm cut out to be the Del Boy of Meli, especially since I will be selling *vlita*. According to Panos, who has a field full of it, *vlita* is very popular. It came as a surprise to me as I've never even heard of the stuff."

"You may not be familiar with the name but you certainly enjoy tucking into it. I do believe it's known as amaranth in English," Marigold said, refreshing my memory by reminding me that summer *horta* is made from simmering these cultivated greens, rather than the wild greens comprising the boiled winter *horta*.

Reflecting on Marigold's words, I conceded she may have a point. I decided to view the next day's activities in a positive light; at least the market part. Panos was offering me a fabulous opportunity to integrate with the Greeks who congregated to sell a wonderful variety of the finest fresh produce. I could appreciate the appeal of such an authentically Greek experience, afforded to few other foreigners. Additionally it would help to cement a solid friendship with Panos.

Recalling that Marigold had spoken of the farmer perhaps having a romantic interest in Violet Burke, I said, "You really think that Panos is interested in my mother, in that way?"

"I do. Spending the day with him tomorrow gives you the perfect opportunity to check out his eligibility as a potential step-father," Marigold said. I rolled my eyes in response; it was a bit of a leap from assuming Panos had a passing interest in Violet Burke to rolling out the welcome mat for him to become a fully paid up member of our family. Really, my wife's matchmaking knew no bounds. "But if she doesn't spurn his advances and they do get serious then someone really must have a quiet word with

Panos about those dreadful wellies of his. I think they must be moulded to his feet."

Marigold's observation made me laugh out loud, until she ruined the moment by adding, "Then again inappropriate footwear does run in the family. One day it will dawn on you that pairing socks with sandals is dreadfully unstylish. I'm still waiting for the penny to drop."

"Pass me my swim shorts. I'll go and change in the Gents and order your drink." I refused to rise to Marigold's bait.

I had an ulterior motive for agreeing to ply my wife with wine; it would loosen her up and lessen the blow when I announced that due to the early start Panos insisted on for the next morning, I would be forced to throw a spanner in Marigold's plans to dine out with the family. A swim and an early night was as much excitement as I could face with the prospect of harvesting a field looming over me. Not overly used to manual labour, I suspected I may well find it back-breaking work. It wouldn't do to appear like a pathetic weakling in front of Panos; I rather think he has at least a good ten years on me.

Strolling across the hot sand to the beach bar, I mused that if my stab at Panos' age was accurate and if Marigold's matchmaking bore fruit, then my mother could well end up with a Greek toy-boy.

By the time I returned to the beach in more suitable attire, Marigold was enjoying a glass of wine, cool drops of condensation dripping from the glass and glistening on her sun-kissed thighs. She was chatting with Elaine who was reclining on an adjacent lounger, whilst Douglas squatted uncomfortably on the sand, supervising the twins' rather messy construction of a sandcastle.

"Uncle Bucket, look at our castle," the girls shouted, dissolving into childish giggles as they pointed out they had made it with a bucket and spade. The pair of them was incapable of keeping their faces straight whenever they uttered the word bucket, even though I'm sure Douglas hadn't shared the sorry tale of my ignominious start in life with them yet.

"Take this," I said offering my half-brother a bottle of high factor sun cream retrieved from the beach bag. "You really should move under the sun umbrella, you don't want to risk burning on top of peeling."

"I think I'll go back into the sea, it will take the sting off," Douglas said, liberally coating his pallid flesh in sun cream.

"I'll come with you, but after a swim I'm afraid I need to be getting back to Meli. I have a ludicrously early start tomorrow, so we'll have to take a rain check on dinner," I said, fully expecting to receive one of Marigold's withering looks for putting a damper on her dinner plans.

"That's fine, dear. I think it's been a long day for everyone," Marigold agreed. Amazingly, I couldn't detect a trace of sarcasm in her voice.

"The girls need an early night too, they've had so much excitement today that they are worn out," Elaine piped up.

"Uncle Bucket, can we bury you in the sand with buckets of sand?" Millie giggled.

"Another time," I humoured her. "Right now I'm off for a swim with your Daddy."

Chapter 12

Sandy Sandwiches

Following a pleasurable dip, Douglas and I minced across the hot as coals sand on our tippy-toes, desperate to avoid singeing our feet, painfully aware that our movements may be interpreted as a tad queer by the bemused onlookers. At least we didn't make an exhibition of ourselves in front of our wives. There was no sign of Marigold, Elaine, or the children, leaving us distinctly perturbed to discover that our beach paraphernalia had been left unattended.

"I expect they've taken the girls to the loo. At least they weren't here to witness our very unmanly trek from the sea," Douglas said, not unduly worried by their absence. Throwing himself on the sand, he said, "It's been such a marvellous day."

I nodded my agreement: apart from the trundling tractor trip down to the coast and the presumed incident of canine murder, the day had gone swimmingly, particularly in light of its wet start.

"I'm so glad that I pursued contact after meeting you at Vic's funeral," Douglas continued. "Elaine thought it was madness, considering I go out of my way to avoid my other two half-brothers, but I had a feeling things would be different with you."

"I'm very glad that you didn't give up on me. I have to say that I am thoroughly enjoying the novelty of having a brother. It's a pity that we missed out on so many years when we could have been developing a brotherly relationship. I'm just sorry this *vlita* nonsense has put a spoke in our getting together tomorrow." My words prompted us to make firm arrangements to meet up on Thursday evening. Although

Thursday was a free day in my diary, I needed to be on hand in Meli during the day, for my mother's arrival.

"Ah, here they come now," Douglas said gesturing as the others appeared, their hands full.

"The girls were hungry, so we got some takeaway toasties from the beach bar," Marigold announced. "It won't make us too late and it will save you the bother of cooking when we get home, Victor. Now, do you fancy cheese and tomato, or cheese and ham?"

Even though tucking into toasties on the beach struck me as a tad insanitary due to the likelihood of sand creating a gritty layer between the bread and the cheese, I was ravenous enough to pounce hungrily on a nicely browned cheese and tomato. In truth I had been staving off hunger pangs ever since Panos had given what I had presumed were my fried sardines to his dog. Whilst Marigold's choice of an impromptu dinner could hardly compare with the delights of fresh *tiganites sardeles,* it would certainly suffice.

"Once we've eaten, you'll need to drive the family back to their hotel, Victor. I'll wait for you here," Marigold said, sending me a withering look as I poked around in my teeth with a finger, extracting gritty grains of sand. "There's no way we can cram the six of us in the Punto all at once."

"It would be sure to violate some Greek road safety law," Douglas sagely nodded.

"Rightio," I agreed, a tad distracted by the sight of a moped pulling into the parking area behind the beach. Whilst we had readily dismissed the notion of attempting to stash six people inside the Punto, it seemed that the owner of the moped had no such trifling reservations, having managed to squash a family of five and what appeared to be half the contents of his house atop his two-wheeled transport. Watching them alight, I made a guess as to the familial relationship, assuming them to be a young couple and their two children. In my mind I relegated the role of children's granny to the middle-aged woman. It was noticeable that the only one not flouting the helmet law was the male driver.

I guessed that the family were local Greeks or Albanians, looking forward to some relaxing beach time at the end of the day. Recalling what the elderly lady in the clinic had said about her foolproof method of identifying Albanians without hearing them speak, I studied the man as closely as distance allowed. Annoyingly, he refused to remove his helmet, thus I was unable to test out the flat head theory. I did speculate that perchance the man was balding beneath his helmet and preferred to keep it on for additional protection against the sun: there again, he may just consider a crash helmet to be more of a masculine fashion statement than a sun hat. I decided it was best not to voice the flat head theory spouted by the pensioner since I rather imagined it was born out of prejudice; some of the local Greeks could be a tad blunt in their opinions about nationals from the neighbouring impoverished country.

Whilst the male of the group disappeared in the direction of the bar, the rest of the family traipsed across the beach, plonking themselves down quite close to us, immediately setting up the folding chairs and the picnic table that had been precariously balanced on the moped. It never ceases to amaze me that with a vast stretch of sand to sit on, some people prefer to encroach on the privacy of others, demonstrating an utter disregard to the polite niceties of social distancing.

The children ran off to paddle in the sea

whilst the two women were preoccupied in setting the stage for a meal. The middle-aged woman shook out an embroidered tablecloth, using her pinny to polish up some cutlery and chivvying the younger woman to unpack a cumbersome carrier bag that I imagined served as their picnic basket.

The children had barely had chance to get wet when the granny bellowed, *"Arianna, Alexandro, ela kai fae,"* calling them to come and eat. In turn the younger woman pulled out a mobile phone, barking instructions, *"Ela Niko, ela kai fae."* I turned away to hide a wry smile: often the local men would be enjoying a drink in the taverna when their womenfolk telephoned, barking orders to summon them home to eat the lovingly prepared meal that awaited them. Not wishing to appear too henpecked in front of the other men, the recipient of the phone call would often ignore the barked orders until his wife impatiently turned up at the taverna, leading him home by the ear. Fortunately, Marigold has never subjected me to such a humiliating scene, most likely because I do most of the cooking.

The tempting aroma of garlic and rosemary wafted over as food was unpacked from Tupperware boxes. Before I could check out what delicious dish they were about to tuck into, the still helmeted man joined them, juggling an awkward windbreaker and a bottle of Amstel. Annoyingly, once the windbreaker was pegged in the sand, my view was completely obscured. Nevertheless, their dining arrangements struck me as a tad more civilised than our pitiful fare of sand infested sandwiches, the crumbs of which were already attracting all manner of revolting beach bugs.

Chapter 13

Milton's Imaginary Stalker

"It is so good to be home, it's been a long day," Marigold yawned when we pulled in to Meli. "I'm glad it will be just the two of us this evening. We can watch the sunset from the roof terrace and then enjoy an early night. I do hope you can manage to get up without waking me tomorrow, I certainly have no desire to see what four in the morning looks like."

"I'm sure you would find it a total novelty,"

I laughed.

Heading up the outdoor staircase, I noticed that Guzim had neglected his putting the chickens to bed duties. Forced to step into the breach, I knew that Marigold would take advantage of my bedding the chickens to sneak back out to the Punto to grab and hide any Marks and Spencer carrier bags of clothing she had snapped up during her shopping expedition with Elaine.

I supposed that my gardener could use the reasonable excuse of suffering a traumatic dog attack for neglecting his duties, especially when coupled with being too sozzled on *ouzo* to stand up straight. Reflecting that it would be the decent thing to at least check up on his welfare, I reluctantly made Guzim a cheese sandwich, remembering his preference for extra onions. Seeming to recall that Guzim's lack of teeth made chewing crusts an impossible task, I duly hacked them off. As I buttered and sliced, I remarked to Marigold that it was a sorry state of affairs that I had dined on toasties on the beach to avoid cooking, but ended up cooking anyway.

"Knocking a sandwich up can hardly be described as cooking, Victor. You do love to talk in hyperbole." The twinkle in Marigold's eyes as she spoke belied any criticism. "Put a bit of that courgette chutney on top of the cheese, it needs using up. I think it's on the turn, the last jar I opened was sprouting mould."

"We've probably kept it too long. There was such a glut of courgettes again that I did make rather a surfeit," I said, thinking that a touch of mould wouldn't do Guzim any harm; indeed, a dose of penicillin may help to prevent a nasty infection taking hold in his bottom. If Guzim got wind of any potential complications, such as sepsis setting in, I could just imagine how he would revel in malingering, being somewhat of a seasoned expert in playing the sympathy card. If Guzim skived off from his chicken duties, it would fall on my unwilling shoulders to clean up their mess; Marigold flatly refused to go near them. No matter how often I assure her that my chickens are clean, she still maintains that they stink.

A cunning plan occurred to me: if Guzim did indulge in a spot of malingering, I could offload the responsibility for the chickens onto Violet Burke once she turned up. My mother is in her element giving the hen house a good bottoming. Thoughts of Vi reminded me that I really needed to work on planting the seed in

Marigold's mind that she would love to invite my mother to move into our downstairs storage. I decided I would turn on the charm after taking Guzim his sandwich.

My culinary efforts were not in vain. Guzim was pathetically grateful for the sandwich, slurring his words in grovelling appreciation. The addition of onion proved to be a stroke of genius since it helped to disguise the overpowering smell of *ouzo*. I was relieved to see that Guzim's pet rabbit, Doruntina, had made its way home, after escaping from the slum of the shed when we deposited what we thought was a dead dog in there. Guzim would have been inconsolable if Kyria Maria had got her hands on his cuddly bed fellow and served it up as *kouneli stifado*.

Leaving Guzim to sleep off the medicinal effects of the *ouzo*, I set to rounding up the chickens, attempting to shoo them into the hen house, no easy task. I thought that Raki was safely inside, but as soon as I turned my back to make a grab for Mavrodafni, Raki ran out and scurried under a shrub. Frustrated that I was no Pied Piper of chickens, I resorted to a spot of bribery, tempting the flock inside with a favourite treat of chopped watermelon.

During a spot of online research into

chicken treats, I had made the appalling discovery that some so-called experts advocate treating one's brood to hard-boiled eggs. It didn't bear thinking about: to my mind it would be encouraging the chickens to engage in disgusting cannibalistic practices that must surely violate every tenet of chicken health and safety law. I made a mental note to do some more research on the issue; I must confess to being rather remiss in keeping up to date with the latest European guidelines since retiring from my illustrious career as a public health inspector.

Only the rooster held out against the watermelon treats, demonstrating that it was no easy pushover. Imagining that perchance it had set its sights on juicier treats, such as Cynthia's frogs, I finally lured it to bed in the hen house with an enticing dollop of courgette chutney. Considering the rooster acts as though it is a cut above the rest of the flock, lording it up at the top of the pecking order, I was surprised when it wolfed down the mouldy chutney with such indiscriminate gusto.

I decided that once the chickens were settled for the night, I would launch my charm offensive on my wife. I planned to ply her with another glass of wine, perhaps even a bottle of the stuff, before dropping some extremely subtle hints about the benefit of having Violet Burke around on a more permanent basis. If I approached the matter in a nuanced enough manner, Marigold would hopefully not cotton on to my efforts to put one over on her.

Even though Marigold had been nagging me for ages about how much we needed either a cleaner or a Roomba, I had resolutely held my ground, refusing to counter such ridiculous extravagance: I had no intention of squandering my hard-earned repping wages on such frivolous luxuries. Instead, I fully intended to turn my mother's enthusiasm for scrubbing to my own advantage, hoping that if I played my cards right Marigold would be the one attempting to persuade me of the benefit of installing Violet Burke and her Vim in our downstairs storage.

Striding towards the house with the intention of sweeping Marigold off her feet, I was instead waylaid by Kyria Maria sticking her head over the garden wall. Without slowing my pace, I bid the black clad old biddy a pleasant evening, only to be stopped dead in my tracks when she complained, "*O methysmenos alvanos eklepse to panteloni tou giou mou.*" I could not believe what I was hearing: she had just accused the drunken Albanian of stealing her son's trousers.

"To ouzo itan farmakeftiko." I assured her the ouzo was medicinal, but Kyria Maria was not buying any of my lame excuses. She launched into a tedious tale about how she had been pegging the washing out first thing that morning, when her chores were interrupted by a visitor. Wishing she would get to the point and skip over the mundane details of serving *tsai tou vounou* to Litsa, I rather abruptly cut my neighbour short, clueless as to what any of this had to do with Guzim. Maria fired a withering look in my direction, proceeding to explain she had thrown Papas Andreas' trousers on the garden wall when she went to greet Litsa. Distracted by other things, she forgot all about the washing until later, by which time the trousers had disappeared, completely vanished into thin air, *"Exafanistike se lepto aera."*

Maria then dropped the bombshell that a couple of hours earlier she had spotted the sozzled Guzim making his way through my garden in Papas Andreas' trousers. Despite her natural tendency to interfere, she had no intention of confronting a drunkard.

"Ti tha kaneis gi afto?" Maria demanded to know what I was going to do about it.

In normal circumstances, mastery of Greek vocabulary allowing, I would demand to know quite why she laboured under the misguided apprehension that it was my responsibility to sort out any shenanigans that Guzim got up to. Due to the severe limitations of my spoken Greek that sentence would most likely come out as, "Why? I am not Guzim's mother." However, as in this instance I was indeed culpable, having given Guzim the supposedly stolen trousers, I recognised that I would need to man up.

"Vrika to panteloni ston kouva. Tous edosa ston Guzim yiati nomiza oti ta petaxate." I was quite emphatic in my defence that I had found the trousers in the bucket and given them to Guzim because I thought she had thrown them away.

"O kouvas?" Kyria Maria questioned, her wrinkled brow furrowed in puzzlement, as though she had never heard the word bucket before.

"Aftos o kados." Pointing to the bucket on the garden wall, I clarified its use as the bartering bucket. *"O kouvas antallagis."*

Throwing her head back and clucking her tongue in disbelief, Maria demanded the trousers back now, *"Thelo to panteloni piso tora."*

Rolling my eyes in exasperation, I marched

back to Guzim's shed. The Albanian would surely think I had lost my marbles when I demanded he return the trousers to me. To make matters worse, the ungrateful wretch hadn't even wanted them in the first place, proclaiming them horrible despite not having a fashionable bone in his body. I could not imagine Papas Andreas being too keen to wear the *ouzo* soaked trousers again if he discovered that after I had accidentally purloined them, Guzim had been prancing round in them.

Fortunately, I was spared an argument with the Albanian shed dweller. Without bothering to knock, I entered his hovel, relieved to see Guzim sprawled on his back, snoring, Doruntina, equally spark out on his chest. Without further ado, I yanked Papas Andreas' trousers off Guzim's prostrate form, an easy task considering they were so loose. I rather expected that Guzim would suffer such a horrendous hangover the next day that he may think the missing trousers were nothing more than a product of his inebriated dreams.

Returning to the garden, I lobbed the offending trousers over the wall. Striding away, I ignored Kyria Maria's strident complaints that the trousers were covered in flea ridden dog hairs and stank of *ouzo*. I was in no mood to get into a slanging match over such mundane trivialities: I needed to be on top form to charm Marigold.

About to step into the downstairs storage to procure a bottle of Lidl red from the ornate wine rack, I was distracted from my mission by the arrival of Dina. She was clutching a bag of something she had picked from the fields to thank me for taking care of Nikoleta. Minus the salutary warning to beware, Dina was the perfect embodiment of the 'Greeks bearing gifts' idiom. Dina's dimples dominated her smiling face, evidence of the delight she felt in surprising me with a gift.

"*Ti einai afto*?" I asked what it was, unfamiliar with the particular type of green vegetation in the bag.

"*Einai vlita.*" Having cleared up the mystery of what *vlita* actually is, Dina gushed that it was very fresh, very delicious, and very good with spring onions and dill, "*Poly fresko, poly nostimo, poly kalo me kremmydakia kai anitho.*"

After thanking Dina profusely for her thoughtful gesture, I asked why she wasn't in the taverna peeling potatoes ready for that evening's chips.

"I Eleni xefloudizei tis patates appose." There was a delightful lilt to Dina's words as she told me that Eleni was peeling the potatoes tonight.

"Bravo." Delighted that Dina was spared the drudgery of the dreary chore for one evening at least, I lifted her off her feet and twirled her around. I wondered if Violet Burke's arrival might also spare Dina the chore of pushing the mop around the taverna: her heart just isn't in it, whereas my mother lives to clean and complain about her swollen feet.

"Me petaxe prin kaneis tin plati sou." Dina's tinkling laughter reverberated as she told me to put her down before I did my back in. Depositing a fond kiss on my cheek, Dina headed off towards the taverna with a skip in her step.

Fishing about in my pocket for the key to the downstairs storage, I balled my fists in frustration when a familiar voice put paid to my imminent plans to launch a charm offensive on my wife.

"I say, old chap, you won't believe what happened today."

"Hello, Milton, what brings you round here?" I said, hoping the tone of my voice conveyed I was in no mood to linger. Recalling that Milton can be terribly slow to take a hint, I added, "I'm afraid I can only spare you a moment, I'm planning a romantic evening with my wife."

"Lucky woman, always a good move to put the effort in to stop things getting stale between us old married couples," Milton boomed.

Wincing at being lumped into the same 'old married couple' category as my much older neighbour, I said, "So tell me, what unbelievable thing happened today?"

"The oddest thing. Norman gave me a lift to the supermarket on the coast, much cheaper than Dina's shop for bulk buying cat food. Anyway, I was just popping in for some tins of…"

"Yes," I said impatiently, wishing he would get to the point. Purchasing cat food hardly struck me as odd considering that Milton and Edna gave house room to more than two dozen strays.

"Well, you could have knocked me down with a feather old chap; I have to say I was taken aback. Bold as brass, she was…"

"Who was, Milton?"

"My stalker." It was news to me that Milton had a stalker, though knowing him I would hazard a guess that he had conjured one up out of his overheated imagination. "She was sitting on a bench on the seafront, with a glass of wine."

"So, what on earth makes you think that a woman drinking wine is stalking you?" I asked. "It sounds like a pretty innocent thing to do."

"Innocent, my foot. She was quite flagrantly reading a copy of 'Delicious Desire.'"

"Did it not occur to you that she may have been a holidaymaker, relaxing with a book, or one of the ex-pats that live on the coast? After all, now that your porn is in print and the odd copy is selling, it can't be a complete surprise to you that someone must be reading it."

"Erotica, old chap, erotica," Milton contradicted me. Porn, smut, erotica, it was all the same to me. I must confess that I was certainly surprised that anyone would willingly be seen reading such salacious material in public, without first taking the precaution of concealing the book in a brown paper bag.

"So, Milton, did this stalker of yours approach you for your autograph?"

My question appeared to confuse Milton, until it suddenly dawned on him that by adopting the pseudonym of Scarlett Bottom he had protected his identity as the actual author.

"Ah, I think I'm getting your drift, old chap."

"The point is that by inventing a pen name, any deranged or obsessed stalkers will be stalking someone that doesn't exist," I said, hoping that the penny had finally dropped.

"Ah, so you're saying she was stalking Scarlett Bottom, not me…"

"Most definitely." I had no intention of wasting my time attempting to convince Milton that there was no stalker and that the whole thing was just a bizarre coincidence.

"Hmm, you've given me something to think about, old chap. Perhaps I did jump to the wrong conclusion, understandable I suppose, first time I've seen anyone reading my published work."

"Take my advice; if you happen to spot anyone with a copy of your book in future, just keep a low profile. Don't go offering to autograph it," I advised, biting my lip to prevent myself from blurting out that any avid porn readers would hardly appreciate being approached by a geriatric pensioner: it was almost a given that Milton would be taken for a dirty old man. "I expect that your readers imagine Scarlett Bottom is a very glamorous woman: in the flesh you may be a bit of a let-down."

"Always rely on you to come up with

sensible advice, Victor, You're right, of course, wouldn't do to burst any bubbles regarding my pseudonym's glamorous image."

Chapter 14

Victor's Charm Offensive

In my desperate haste to escape from Milton before he could bore me rigid with yet more inane ramblings about imaginary stalkers, I completely forgot to dig out a bottle of red from the downstairs storage. With no wine in hand to lubricate my wife, my charm offensive was off to a feeble start when I joined her on the roof terrace. Since I had been such an age with the chickens and intruders, Marigold had primped and preened by showering and changing.

Fortunately, she didn't appear to have noticed that the twins had emptied her expensive bottle of Rive Gauche shower gel over the cats; she must have stood downwind of her precious felines. I made a mental note to douse Clawsome and Catastrophe in the contents of one of the particularly pungent bottles of aftershave I had inherited with the house, to put Marigold off the scent. Spiros' uncle had been in the habit of hoarding cheap aftershave before he met his untimely demise, plummeting from the roof.

"You do look lovely, darling," I complimented my wife. "Is that a new frock?"

"What, this old thing? I've had it forever. Really, Victor, if you ever bothered to notice what I am wearing you would realise that you've seen me in this dress countless times before."

"Let me just give you a hand to remove the label," I offered, snapping off the tell-tale purchase tag dangling from her back neckline. Mortified by her oversight, Marigold made a grab for her fan. Unfolding it, she frantically began to fan herself, using it as a convenient way of covering her guilty blushes.

"I swear it's getting hotter up here rather than cooler," she sighed, hastily changing the subject.

"It's the humidity. Why not join me in selecting a bottle of red in the downstairs storage? It will be much cooler down there," I invited.

"Hardly much of a selection to choose from, Victor. I thought all the wine you stashed down there was cheapish plonk from Lidl," Marigold pointed out.

"There may be the odd bottle of something a tad more sophisticated," I said with about as much conviction as Marigold had mustered when denying she was wearing a new dress. As far as I could recall, most of the wine on hand had been snapped up on special during one of Lidl's *Souper Savato* offers. "Come on," I encouraged, extending my hand, delighted when Marigold slipped hers into mine.

"It's been an age since I've been in here," Marigold said as we stepped into the cool and dusty storage space. "It's rather become yours and Barry's place to get away from it all. Perhaps we should rename it the Man Cave."

"No need for that, dear, I have my office," I said, unfolding a deckchair for Marigold. "Take a pew while I dig out some glasses and a bottle of red."

Relaxing in the deckchair, Marigold studied

the space with renewed interest. "Did you know that in Greek this kind of storage space below the house is typically known as an *apothiki*?"

"The word rings a bell…ah; I seem to recall an *apothiki* is a warehouse."

"Well, we do warehouse all our junk in here," Marigold said.

"It certainly has a more upmarket ring to it than downstairs storage. We must make a toast to re-christening the area the *apothiki,*" I suggested, attempting to yank a stubborn cork out of the bottle.

"The *apothiki* is certainly lovely and cool; if the place wasn't filled with junk it would be tempting to bring the bed down," Marigold said. "Oh, do pass that to me, Victor. You'd think by now you could master a basic corkscrew. I can see why you have a preference for screw top wine."

Overlooking Marigold's slur on my competence with a corkscrew, I handed over the bottle, making a mental note to stash a lever type corkscrew down here for future openings. The cork popped out with a satisfying plop and Marigold returned the bottle to me for pouring.

"Take this, it's a cheeky little number from Chile," I said, presenting her with a glass of red.

"Not from Lidl?"

"From Chile, via Lidl. It's certainly an improvement on that plastic red from the local shop." Tina had invested in a batch of acidic red wine that had the misfortune to taste as cheap as it cost: it wouldn't surprise me if the wine corroded the plastic bottles that housed it.

"*Yamas.*"

"*Yamas,*" Marigold cheered, raising her glass. "Well, if we have any of that plastic wine still lying around, palm it off on Barry. Since it tastes like vinegar it will be right up his alley." In truth Barry had become quite addicted to the bizarre combination of vinegar and honey that he originally quaffed as a supposed local remedy for travel sickness, clueless to the fact that the local ladies were amusing themselves by teasing him with a fabricated cure. Still, it had done the trick. Barry rarely suffers from motion sickness these days and he's done a marvellous job of overcoming his vertigo; just as well since his job often involves scrambling up precarious scaffolding.

"Just two more evenings alone before Violet Burke takes over the spare room," I said, subtly introducing my mother into our conversation. "I do hope her presence won't put you out too much."

"Don't worry, Victor, I can tolerate your mother in small doses. I find it quite easy to tune her out when she chunters on about chip fat and swollen feet. After all, I've had plenty of years of practice being married to you and having to tune out all those mind-numbing lectures about tedious pathogens and different strains of mould." Marigold's lips curled in amusement as she spoke, but I still felt the sting of her words, being a tad sensitive to accusations of droning on. I bit my tongue. Starting an argument would do nothing to further the cause I had in mind.

"One thing I am looking forward to is the way that Vi will insist on giving the house a good bottoming," Marigold continued. "Since you flatly refuse to let me hire a woman that does or splash out on a Roomba, your mother is the next best thing. I do find housework such a chore in this heat, while Vi seems to positively revel in it."

"Whilst I would never criticise your efforts in the cleaning department, I know your heart isn't in it. Mother does have the knack of giving the place a thoroughly hygienic bottoming," I agreed.

"She's certainly a stickler for removing

every last mosquito corpse from under the beds," Marigold chuckled. "Don't forget to sound Panos out tomorrow; I'm certain he's pretty sweet on your mother. I'm expecting you to encourage him."

"Well, if your matchmaking antennae are on point then it's a pity that nothing is likely to come of it."

"What makes you say that?" Marigold raised a questioning eyebrow whilst sipping her wine. "I think they make an ideal match. Surely you aren't going to get all precious about your mother having a gentleman caller."

"Considering the stream of men she's had in the past, I'm hardly likely to start vetting any potential suitors. It's not that, I think that long distance relationships are doomed to fail when the couple are incapable of communicating in the same language. I can just see Panos attempting to whisper sweet nothings down a long distance phone line and Violet Burke hanging up on him, mistaking him for a heavy breather," I said.

"Even though they rub along nicely when they are together, you may have a point about the difficulties of making it work long distance. It proved a flop between Geraldine and Papas

Andreas in the end, and he at least has a bit of English..."

"He's also a celibate cleric who isn't meant to be engaging in illicit assignations with a foreign woman," I pointed out, recollecting that Papas Andreas was still clueless that he had been cast on the scrapheap of love and that Geraldine was walking out with a new fellow.

"It's just as well that things seem to be working out between Geraldine and that venereal disease chap..."

"Sexually transmitted infections," I corrected, cringing inwardly at the way Marigold so casually used such a tactless and incendiary phrase: she knows full well that I dislike having any unnecessary reminders of being abandoned in a bucket flung in my face. Personally, I rather hoped that Geraldine's latest victim was just another passing phase. I certainly didn't want her dragging an expert in sexually transmitted infections over to Meli for a holiday. I could only imagine how mortifying it would be if he insisted on talking shop over the dinner table.

"I suppose if things do look promising between Vi and Panos, then we must encourage your mother to spend more time over here," Marigold suggested. I could have whooped with delight at my wife's words, but instead adopted an expression of complete indifference. I had no intention of appearing like a pushover. I needed Marigold to convince herself that it was her idea to move Violet Burke to Meli. I would need to appear a tad reluctant so that Marigold could talk me round.

"I'm not sure if it's a good idea to have my mother cluttering up the spare room on a long-term basis," I said, hoping Marigold would take the hint and suggest converting the *apothiki* into a living space.

"But it won't be long-term, Victor. Once Panos proposes then Violet Burke can move in with him."

My jaw dropped at the warped way Marigold's mind works. To the best of my knowledge, Panos and Violet Burke had only shared a couple of incommunicable, indecipherable conversations, yet my wife was already marrying them off.

"We'll have to find somewhere to put her whilst Panos does his courting," I hastily pointed out. "I expect he's rather set in his ways after being on his own for so long."

"Is he divorced or widowed?" Marigold asked.

"I haven't a clue," I admitted.

"Really Victor, you spend enough time with the fellow. What on earth do you talk about?"

"Well, chickens mostly. And vegetables, of course. We did attempt a conversation about soil drainage but it got a tad confusing, I rather think we were at cross purposes. Panos seemed to be under the impression that I had a bit of a problem with the septic tank."

My words provoked one of Marigold's withering looks. Seriously, did the woman really expect Greek men to sit around discussing their feelings and other such gumpf? Admittedly, Spiros and Barry often confide in me about their love lives, seeking out my advice, but Panos is of another generation.

"Never mind, I will get Athena to fill me in on any of Panos' past romantic entanglements at the party tomorrow," Marigold said. "I will leave it to you to sound out his prospects to ensure he can support your mother…"

"In the manner to which she is accustomed to," I interrupted. "I think it's a pretty safe bet that with all his fields of potatoes, Panos will be able to keep my mother in chips."

"Really, Victor, is there any need for such sarcasm?" Marigold said before reverting to the topic of where to put Violet Burke whilst she was wooed by the welly wearing farmer.

"Victor, whilst it may be true that your mother is growing on me, I'm not sure that I want her taking up the spare bedroom for more than a week or two. It will definitely cramp our style having a cantankerous pensioner tagging along wherever we go. You know how she loathes Greek food; she'll make us a laughing stock by demanding Fray Bentos steak and kidney pies in Greek tavernas and complaining that all the food is too oily."

"The longer she spends in Meli, the less dependent on us she'll be. Now that she is making friends of her own in the area, she won't be so reliant on our company. The last time she visited she spent a lot of her time next door with Kyria Maria," I said. "It would probably suit Vi best if she had her own space for independent living."

"It's a pity that Guzim is so attached to his shed, with a bit of work…"

"Yes, well, the point is moot, Guzim is not for shifting. He's very attached to his personal bit of Greek real estate. Now, if only there was somewhere else we could put Violet Burke, where she wouldn't get under our feet."

I adopted a thoughtful expression whilst surveying the space we were in with deliberate vagueness. I could almost see the cogs in my wife's brain turning as Marigold followed my gaze, her eyes narrowing as she studied the *apothiki* thoughtfully. Any minute now, I thought, crossing my fingers.

Marigold opened her mouth to speak, clamping it shut again as she changed her mind. Although the suggestion to convert the *apothiki* into living quarters was on the tip of her tongue, I realised that she still had reservations. Since I still had a few reservations of my own, I could empathise with her reluctance, but my thought processes were further along. I felt a tad miffed that I could no longer pull the old 'only living relative' sympathy card out of my hat for leverage, but the discovery of three half-brothers had rather made that line a tad redundant.

"We could always do something with this space, Victor. Remember, we did consider converting it into a separate abode for Barry, until Cynthia flatly refused to live underneath us."

"Gosh, I'd forgotten all about that," I fibbed. "It never even crossed my mind that we could put my mother down here. Certainly the place has potential..."

"Heaps of potential and just think how your mother's swollen feet will appreciate being on ground level," Marigold gushed with more than a hint of excitement in her voice. "I must stock up on some interior design magazines for inspiration."

"You have such an eye for stylish décor," I flattered my wife. "I suppose we could ask Barry to pop over and give his thoughts on dividing the space into rooms."

"I can see the advantages of installing your mother down here," Marigold continued. "She'd be on hand to see to the cats if we fancied an impromptu night away, and Kyria Maria would probably visit her down here rather than barging into our kitchen. But there are downsides too; converting it would be terribly noisy…not to mention the mess. It would involve much more work than we had done upstairs, there's not even a bathroom down here."

Worried that Marigold was on the verge of changing her mind, I recklessly threw in a bribe.

"I shall whisk you away on a luxury mini-break while the builders are in." The mere mention of an unexpected mini-break brought a twinkle to Marigold's eyes.

"If we do turn it into separate quarters, it

would be very handy when other guests visit. It was a terrible squash upstairs when we had everyone over for Barry's wedding," Marigold enthused. "I'm sure the twins would love their own space…when they're in their teens they may want to fly over to stay with their Aunty and Uncle Bucket."

"Indeed," I agreed, nodding sagely, not bothering to point out that Marigold was skipping ahead a good decade in her planning. "We could even consider letting it out as holiday accommodation to bring in some extra cash."

The twinkle in Marigold's eyes disappeared at such an audacious suggestion on my part.

"You can think again, Victor. Do you really imagine that I'm prepared to clean up after mucky tourists? I'm having nothing to do with it."

"We can get a woman in to clean," I rashly declared.

"Oh, so it's okay to get a woman in to clean up after some random tourists who might put some cash in your pocket, but when I wanted us to get a cleaner in, you put your foot down," Marigold complained.

Not wishing to shoot myself in the aforementioned foot, I dropped all mention of tourists potentially renting our downstairs storage.

"Well, if my mother is in Meli on a more permanent basis, I can give her a bit of pocket money to clean upstairs and you can put your feet up. You know that I'd like to help her out more financially, but she's too proud to accept a handout."

"You know full well that Vi doesn't like to be thought of as a charity case," Marigold reminded me.

"She can be incredibly stubborn. You mustn't think that I don't want a cleaner because I'm a total Scrooge. I really don't like the idea of a stranger poking round in the house," I said. As a person who values my privacy, the idea of someone coming into our home and rummaging through our things held no appeal: perish the thought that some nosey parker cleaning woman might uncover the first draft of my moving to Greece book and reveal V.D. Bucket's true identity, or that she might discover Harold's stash of Grecian 2000 in the bathroom cabinet and spread malicious rumours that I touch up my grey. "At least we know where we are with my mother, she is honest and not one for gossip."

"That's a good point; the thought of a loose lipped cleaner does make me uneasy," Marigold admitted, making me ponder what secrets she didn't want getting out. "And if I'm honest, I suppose I would feel the need to clean up before a daily woman came in, she might be judgemental. I wouldn't need to bother for Vi's benefit. She already thinks I have lax standards in comparison to her impossibly exacting notion of cleanliness."

"I expect that Dina could be persuaded to take Violet Burke on to do a spot of cleaning in the taverna too," I said. "You know how Dina detests slopping the mop around and how she has to be constantly reminded to give the toilet a good bleaching."

"I'm sure that you could persuade Dina to do anything, she worships the ground you walk on," Marigold teased. Topping up Marigold's glass, I deposited a kiss on her cheek.

"I'm a lucky man to have you as my wife, darling. Cynthia turns green every time anyone mentions how much Litsa adores Barry; it's a bit of a sore point with her. Your lack of such petty jealousy makes me appreciate you all the more."

"Dina's a sweetheart. You do get a sight more mothering from her than you do from

Violet Burke."

"Very true." The two women were like chalk and cheese, Dina warm and motherly, Violet Burke bossy and bulbous.

"I happen to think that your mother cleaning at the taverna is an excellent idea, a part time job will keep her occupied and out of our hair. Like you said, it will put some money in her pocket, she's going to miss what she earns at the chippy," Marigold stated. "Not to mention the place could certainly benefit from a thorough scrubbing. Even though the food is excellent, I do sometimes despair that we are forced to eat in such filthy surroundings."

"So, shall I have a word with Barry about converting this place into a self-contained granny flat for Violet Burke?"

"Considering how loathe you usually are to let the moths out of your wallet, you seem awfully keen," Marigold said, her voice carrying the first hint of suspicion that she had been manipulated.

"Barry is sure to give us a good discount," I declared. "I'll give him a call; let him know that you are keen on converting this place for Violet Burke to move into."

"It's funny Victor, until this evening I never

gave so much as a thought to the possibility of your mother being out here on anything like a permanent basis," Marigold said, looking a tad bewildered by the speed of her decision.

"Well, you've managed to persuade me to the merits of your idea, darling," I said. "Here, let me top your glass up."

"I shouldn't really; I'm beginning to feel a bit squiffy."

"Just another drop," I encouraged, hoping that Violet Burke would prove to be as malleable as Marigold. I really would feel more at ease once my mother was installed downstairs rather than in some ghastly high rise on a crime ridden estate.

Chapter 15

Body of a Greek God

It was the second consecutive morning that I was up and about long before the first hint of dawn. The previous day's mission of ridding my outdoor spa of any random frogs before Marigold could discover their presence struck me as a more pressing incentive to rise from my bed than the decidedly grim prospect of toiling in Panos' field before first light.

Considering the sweaty labours awaiting me, showering seemed a tad unnecessary, yet nevertheless I maintained my rigorous hygiene standards by shivering under barely a trickle of lukewarm water. Venturing down the slippery slope of letting one's standards slip invariably puts one on the path to unsociable body odour and the disgraceful habit of wandering about in smelly unwashed clothes: one need look no further than Guzim for a walking example of such slovenly practices.

The electric water pump groaned in noisy protest, siphoning water from the back-up tank to the shower, alerting me that the village water supply, always precarious, was off yet again. I crossed my fingers that the din from the pump wouldn't wake Marigold: I would never hear the end of it if her beauty sleep was rudely disturbed at such an unspeakable hour. I made a mental note to check on the water level in the tank to determine if I must put my foot down and implement strict rationing once again.

In light of Violet Burke's impending visit this was a most inconvenient time to run out of water. Thoughts of my mother made me ponder the likelihood of her indulging in my outdoor spa. One of her constant complaints when she visited was the lack of a bathtub, resulting in one of my constant gripes; the way she insisted on soaking her swollen feet in my washing up bowl. Fortunately the outdoor bath tub had been craftily hidden from Kyria Maria's prying eyes by the new grape arbor. Concealment of said tub was crucial. If my neighbour got wind of it she may well mistake it for a swimming pool: once in, she might well refuse to ever get out. I reasoned that even if Violet Burke spilled the beans to her bosom companion next door, Maria wouldn't have a clue what she was talking about due to their inability to make sense of each other's mother tongues.

Since my style leans more towards formal than casual attire, my wardrobe is a tad bereft of suitable clothing for manual labour. Wishing that I'd had the foresight to borrow some overalls from Barry, I selected my oldest fawn slacks and paired them with Barry's latest Christmas offering. My brother-in-law likes to imagine he is being ironic by deliberately gifting me something he knows I would never be caught dead wearing, in this instance a garish tee-shirt emblazoned with the rather misleading slogan, 'Body of a Greek God.' Barry knows full well it will do nothing but attract moths at the back of my wardrobe since I always insist on wearing a button-down shirt.

Even though the Christmas offering evoked a snort of derision from Marigold, she still managed to accuse me of being ungrateful and unfestive when I refused to don it during the holiday. Taking my lead from Panos, I completed the look with a pair of green wellies, fully expecting the farmer to come out with some disparaging remark about how I'd obviously never got my feet dirty judging by their pristine condition.

Gulping down a strong coffee, I fed the cats and hastily penned a note to Marigold asking her to let the chickens out of the henhouse if Guzim was too hungover to crawl out of his shed. The rooster's chorus announced the advent of dawn, a raucous and timely reminder that I needed to be making tracks. There was a welcome chill in the air when I hit the street; the day wouldn't begin to warm up until sunrise. Meli was perfectly still as I made my way to Panos' place, the path illuminated by a silvery sky.

A feline figure streaked past me; I recognised it as Cynthia's vile cat, Kouneli, no doubt out on its nightly prowl of rape and pillage. The peace was shattered by feline screeching and hissing, leading me to suspect that Kouneli had come upon some hapless prey. The defensive hissing din indicated the intended victim had no intention of succumbing to Kouneli, unwilling to roll over and submit to being the predator's latest conquest. I was relieved that Catastrophe and Clawsome were safely tucked up at home out of harm's way, and grateful that Pickles had not inherited his father's disgraceful habits.

The lamp above Panos' back door cast a yellow glow, serving as a welcome beacon. Apollo unleashed a blood-curdling howl as I sidestepped him, holding my breath. The guard dog instantly settled down at a word from its master. I was greatly relieved to see that the solid looking chain purchased by Spiros had replaced the frayed rope. The beast would need to be a veritable Houdini to break free of its shiny new shackle.

"Kalimera Victor, ela mesa. Theleis proino?" Panos greeted me at the door, raising his unruly eyebrows in bemusement when he clocked my pristine green wellies. Ushering me inside, he asked if I wanted breakfast. Knowing that most Greeks tend to skip the most important meal of the day in favour of a mid-morning cheese or spinach pie, I imagined that the proposed breakfast would comprise a cardiac inducing offering

of a cigarette and a tumbler of *raki*.

"Den kapnizo kai apofevgo ta dynata pnevmata to proi," I quipped, telling Panos that I don't smoke and that I avoid strong spirits first thing in the morning.

"Afto einai asteio. Kathiste, mageirevo avga yia proino." Howling with laughter, Panos said that was funny. He told me to sit down; he was cooking eggs for breakfast.

Pulling out a chair, I welcomed anything that delayed the start of the working day. The idea of toiling in the fields was no more alluring than when Panos had first threatened it. The farmer deposited a plate of toasted bread in front of me, topping it with two fried eggs served directly from the frying pan. As lashings of olive oil soaked into the toast, Panos garnished my eggs with a sprinkle of oregano and filled my coffee cup with a strong brew from the *briki*.

"Thes raki ston kafe sou?" Before I had chance to decline the offer of *raki* in my coffee, Panos instructed me to tuck into my breakfast, laughing that I was way too easy to wind-up and that the last thing he needed on his hands was an inebriated ex-public health inspector. Ignoring Panos' observation, I duly tucked into the food,

telling Panos I would need all my strength once he put me to work.

Using the back of his hand to wipe a dribble of yolk from his chin, Panos erupted in laughter, once again repeating his assertion that I was a pushover in the wind-up department.

"Den yparchei douleia, meta to proino pigainoume stin agora," Panos declared.

I stared at the farmer in confusion, not quite sure which one of us was losing the plot. If my translation skills were firing on all cylinders then Panos had just informed me that there was no field work to do; after breakfast we would go to the market.

"Ti ginetai me to vlita?" I said, asking what about the *vlita*.

"To poulame stin agora." Panos confirmed we would sell it at the market.

Sipping our coffees we engaged in a somewhat convoluted and rather ridiculous conversation, which for clarity I will pen in English.

"Why did you tell me that we'd be harvesting *vlita*?" I asked.

"To wind you up," Panos laughed. "Seriously, Victor, can you to imagine you'd be of any practical use in the fields? I have it on the good authority that your wife has to rely on her brother to do anything manual around the house. I'd like to know the last time you got your hands dirty on the job, you are forever faffing about with a bottle of hand sanitiser."

"There's no need to poke fun at my habit of keeping germs at bay. My current line of work involves lots of meeting and greeting. One can never be too careful when it comes to endlessly shaking hands. Anyway, since we're not harvesting, why did you insist on such an early start?"

"To get the decent breakfast inside you before the off. It is the heavy work loading all the *vlita, nectarinia* and *patates* to sell at the market. Once we arrive we have to unload everything. I suppose you think that our wares hop onto the stall and display themselves."

Groaning inwardly at the thought of the long trip to town in the bone-rattling tractor, I said, "Well, I'm glad you were able to derive such amusement from making me the butt of your jokes."

"But naturally I had the ulterior motive for deceiving you into thinking you would be harvesting the fields," Panos continued.

"An ulterior motive?" I queried.

"Yes, the definitely. I knew it was the only

way to stop you turning up at the market and sticking out like the sore thumb in the shirt and tie. With you standing alongside me looking like the dog's breakfast, my customers would likely mistake you for the tax inspector and give their business to rival stallholders."

"I rather think you mean a dog's dinner," I corrected, no easy task considering his original words were uttered in Greek. "The term 'a dog's breakfast' refers to something messy, I think you meant that if I turned up in more formal attire, I would look like the dog's dinner."

"Breakfast, dinner, it is all the same to me, Victor, the dog is not the fussy about the meal. I just wanted you to be the dress down so that you would fit in amongst the simple market folk. By the way, what does it to say on your tee-shirt?"

"It says, 'Body of a Greek God.'"

"In your dreams, Victor." As Panos' howls of laughter disturbed Apollo, the dog joined in, matching his master's howls. Finally composing himself somewhat, Panos said, "I like that you can to laugh at yourself, Victor. Only someone with the sense of irony could hope to carry off such the tee-shirt."

Chapter 16

To Market We Go

Whilst it would only be natural to be a tad irritated that Panos had lured me to his farm before first light under false pretences, I was instead immensely relieved that I would not be getting all down and dirty in the fields, harvesting *vlita.* Although I was less than amused that Panos had suckered me into wearing such a dreadful outfit in public, I pragmatically reasoned there was nothing to be done about it; Panos insisted we must set off for the market the moment our cargo of fruit and vegetables was loaded.

Stepping outside, there was just enough light to discern an enormous pile of hessian sacks brimming with the produce we needed to sell. My back groaned in protest at the prospect of loading the sacks onto the transport and I made a feeble attempt to flex my muscles in readiness. Looking around, I noticed there was no sign of the tractor. Fervently hoping I would not be expected to carry the sacks to wherever Panos had parked the bone rattling machine, I asked him where it was. *"Pou einai to trakter?"*

I was rather taken aback when Panos responded that we didn't need the tractor as we were driving to market in his pick-up, a pick-up I had been ignorant existed until that moment. *"Den chreiazomaste to trakter, pigainoume stin agora sti pick-up."*

Leading the way to an area at the back of his yard, Panos proceeded to toss some wooden pallets to one side. The pallets had effectively served as a makeshift barrier, cleverly concealing a shiny black pick-up in pristine condition. Having never seen Panos behind the wheel of anything other than his ancient tractor, I was gobsmacked by the unveiling of this modern machine. Marigold would surely approve that the welly wearing farmer had more suitable wheels than tractor ones for ferrying my mother. For my own part, I could feel the bones in my body almost jumping for joy to be spared the rattling ride up to town in the cumbersome and clattering old tractor.

Shrugging off my question about why he didn't use this spanking new vehicle to get around Meli, Panos gestured towards the sacks, indicating there was work to be done. Attempting to heave a giant sack of spuds onto the cargo bed, I came close to giving myself a hernia. Clocking my rather feeble performance, Panos clucked his tongue disparagingly, relieving me of my burden as though it weighed no more than a bag of feathers. A tad embarrassed to be outmuscled by a pension aged fellow with a good ten years on me, I accepted his direction to concentrate on loading the sacks of salad leaves. Even though the bags of *vlita* were relatively light, I threw in the odd exaggerated groan to convince Panos that I was pulling my weight.

Once the cargo bed was loaded with sacks of potatoes, nectarines and *vlita,* Panos added a couple of crates of plump juicy tomatoes and a large basket full of freshly laid eggs. Considering he made no effort to wrap each egg individually or to pop them into cardboard cartons designed for the purpose, I marvelled at his confidence in transporting such delicate cargo on potholed roads. I was almost tempted to place a wager as to how many eggs would survive the journey without cracking.

Panos climbed up amongst his wares on the cargo deck to check his stock before the off. Hoisting a sack of potatoes onto his shoulder, he dropped them back in the yard, announcing they were the best of the crop and he would give them to Violeta. Noting how he had Grekified my mother's name, I nodded amiably, not sure how Violet Burke would react to the name change or how she would feel about being wooed with potatoes. I rather think Marigold may have dropped me for a more attractive proposition if I'd presented her with a bag of spuds as a token of my affections back in our courting days.

Whilst the cab in Panos' tractor resembled a dustbin on wheels, the pick-up cab was neat and clean, the leather seats still encased in their original plastic wrapping. I couldn't resist asking Panos why he hadn't used this vehicle to transport Guzim to the clinic, not too surprised when he responded, *"Den ithela Alvaniko aima se oles tis theseis."* In translation this means he didn't want Albanian blood all over the seats. I couldn't be bothered to point out the obvious: Guzim's blood would have had its work cut out seeping through the plastic protection.

With a ninety-minute journey ahead of us there was plenty of opportunity to practice my conversational Greek. Since Panos does not speak a word of English, I would not be able to rest on my laurels and slip into lazy habits like I do when I'm in the company of Greeks eager to practice their English. For the ease of my readers though, I will parse our ensuing dialogue in English.

"The Greece are the playing the tomorrow," Panos said, striking up a conversation.

"Playing what?" I asked.

"The football, Victor," Panos replied, sending me a withering look that I felt was a tad unnecessary. My question didn't strike me as so outrageous considering Greece as a nation must surely engage in other sports beside football; after all I had noticed a tennis court down on the coast and basketball hoops adorning the children's playgrounds.

"It is the UEFA semi-final, we will to

slaughter the Czech Republic," Panos said.

"I don't take much interest in football," I admitted. Panos' face reflected a look of sheer disbelief at this blatant sacrilege, making me feel like an atheist confessing to a vicar that I don't attend church. His disapproval prompted me to hastily clarify, "But naturally I will support Greece in tomorrow's match."

"You will to cheer on the Greece in the taverna?" I couldn't quite gauge from Panos' tone if his statement was a question or an order.

"I won't be able to make it. I have arranged to meet my brother and his family down on the coast tomorrow evening," I said, grateful for a convenient get-out-clause. Hoping to avoid a tedious lecture on football, I recalled Marigold's insistence that I press Panos about his intentions regarding Violet Burke and subtly introduced my mother into the conversation.

"My mother flies into Athens tomorrow."

"A fine woman, very handsome," Panos declared, finger-combing his moustache as though in preparation for impressing Violet Burke with his rather bristle-like facial hair. Our small talk dried up rather abruptly, Panos seemingly reluctant to declare his feelings for my mother. Imagining Marigold's frustration if I allowed the subject to wither, I pressed on.

"My mother is looking forward to Anastasia's baptism. I take it you'll be there."

"I not to do the church, there is too much the farm work in the mornings. I will to go to the party. Will the Marigold to cook the idiocy?"

Rather taken aback by Panos' nonsensical question, I was lost for words. Panos continued, saying, "Your wife's idiocy is to like eating the bowl of the cream heaven."

I remained flummoxed until he added, "I like very much the sherry in the cake."

Realisation slowly dawned: Panos was referring to Marigold's rather scrumptious sherry trifle. Upon hearing the farmer use the Greek word *sachlamara,* I had mentally translated its meaning to idiocy: a quick flick through my ever present pocket dictionary revealed that *sachlamara* could also be used to refer to a trifle, not a trifle in the creamy dessert sense, but a trifle in the sense of something trivial. At some point after indulging in a bowl of my wife's excellent dessert, Panos must have asked what it was called and got his wires crossed in translation. For Panos' benefit I clarified that an English trifle remains a trifle in Greek, but he was welcome to pronounce the English word with a strong

Greek accent.

"In her role of godmother, Athena is organising the party, but I'm sure that I can persuade Marigold to whip up a trifle. I will tell her how much you enjoy it," I said. Whilst it is true that many of the Greek villagers are reluctant to sample foreign food, my wife's trifle is universally praised in Meli as a superlative masterpiece of jelly, sponge and custard. Marigold would definitely be up for creating her famous dessert if it would help to entice Panos along to the baptism party as bait for my mother, but she would be less than impressed if I revealed that the farmer had expressed altogether more enthusiasm for her trifle than he did for her mother-in-law.

We were making good progress in the pick-up, the mountain roads practically deserted at this early hour. The sun had risen and it promised to be another beautiful day. Panos pointed out some wild carrot flowers in an olive grove that we passed. He voiced his regret that he hadn't thrown the odd goat in the back of the pick-up, explaining that his goats enjoyed carrot flowers as much as he enjoyed Marigold's trifle.

I was quite looking forward to my stint behind a market stall; it would give me the opportunity to mingle in an authentically Greek setting. When Panos told me that his stall was situated in the outdoor rather than indoor market, I was a tad concerned about coping with the heat. I sighed in relief when he assured me the stall was sited beneath a sun canopy.

Panos and I fell into a companionable silence, frustrated by another futile attempt to discuss soil drainage. Reflecting that Marigold would be most put out by my failure to grill Panos about his intentions towards my mother, I decided to have one last shot at getting the farmer to open up about his feelings for Violet Burke.

"So, are you looking forward to spending time with my mother during her visit?"

"The Violeta is the fine woman, Victor. Unlike you the English, I am not the man to discuss the feelings," Panos shot me down me with a strained look. I knew how he felt: I certainly felt awkward bringing the subject up in the first place. I decided that if Marigold was so desperate for information, she could grill Panos herself at the baptism party.

An awkward silence followed as we took the final downward stretch to town, only broken by the trilling ring of my mobile. I hoped that it wasn't Marigold phoning to demand details about Panos' feelings for my mother, but then I realised it was still too absurdly early for my wife to be up.

"You're up early," I greeted my brother-in-law.

"The baby got me up at the crack of dawn," Barry said, yawning down the phone line.

"I'm glad you've phoned. Marigold is keen to convert the *apothiki* into a granny flat.

"The apo what?" Barry stuttered.

"The downstairs storage."

"Ah, so you've sold her on your grand design, *bravo*."

"Marigold thinks it was her brilliant idea. Make sure that you play along and don't let on that I was planning it all along," I said.

"Rightio, mum's the word, your secret is safe with me. Much better if we let the women in our lives think that they make the decisions," Barry laughed. I smiled at his words. I was a lucky man indeed to have a brother-in-law so willing to take my side and not rat me out to his sister. "You owe me one, Victor."

"Anything," I rashly promised.

"Well, as it happens, I want some tripe. I heard you were going to be at the market today so I thought you could have a good scout round the meat stalls and see if you can't turn up a nice piece of honeycomb," Barry wheedled. "Last night I had a real craving for a nice bit of tripe served up with raw onions, lashings of malt vinegar and chips, but Tina didn't have any at the shop. I'm sure they must sell it in Greece though, Victor, otherwise why would they bother inventing a Greek word for it. I can't remember what it is, but I know there is one."

"*Patsas.*" The Greek word for tripe tripped off my tongue, even as my stomach recoiled at Barry's vile habit of eating raw tripe. For as long as I've known him, my brother-in-law has had rather a penchant for this northern delicacy. I imagine it must be an acquired taste, but one I certainly have no desire to acquire. During my illustrious career as a public health inspector, I had encountered many a chef attempting to turn cheap cuts of offal into something edible, bestowing pretentious names on their concoctions. They clearly hoped to detract attention from the fact that they were serving up the internal scrapings of detritus from the carcass in order to slap a high price tag on the cheapest cuts.

"Hold on a sec, Barry. I'm with Panos. I'll ask him if they are likely to sell tripe at the market."

After conferring with Panos, I reported back to Barry. "Panos says they sell tripe at the market, apparently it's very popular in a soup the Greeks eat as a hangover cure. Funnily enough they call it *patsas* rather than *patsas soupia.*"

"I don't want the nasty looking stuff you have to cook, Victor. I want the honeycomb tripe that I can eat raw."

After another confab with Panos, I reported back to Barry. "Panos hasn't got a clue what I'm on about. It's not easy attempting to describe honeycomb tripe, he's got it into his head that I'm after the stomach of a cow that's been reared on an exclusive diet of honey."

"A cow's stomach is a cow's stomach. I doubt that Greek cows come with their very own unique digestive system," Barry argued.

"Leave it with me, Barry. I'll take a wander round the meat stalls and see if I can spot some," I promised.

At least Barry's desire for tripe had broken the uneasy silence between Panos and me. Panos spent the rest of our journey enthusing about the wonders of *patsas*. Whilst I was familiar with the Greek words for fish taverna, *psarotaverna,* and grill-house, *psistaria,* I had never heard of a *patsazidiko,* until Panos explained it was a taverna specialising in popular tripe soup.

I came very close to losing my breakfast eggs when Panos delved into great detail, describing the various internal organs and hooves that were simmered for hours to create the traditional hangover cure. I had never encountered this soup during my time in Greece; fortunately it didn't feature on Nikos' menu which never varies from his staples of cheese, salad, chips and grilled meat. Panos was gobsmacked to learn that I had lived in Greece for almost two years without tasting the soup. He promised to remedy my culinary ignorance by cooking up a pan of the stuff. I made a mental note to steer well clear of Panos' kitchen for the foreseeable.

Refusing to let the subject drop, Panos insisted that I must have come across a similar soup, the traditional Greek Easter dish of *mayiritsa,* an offal based lemon and rice soup served after the midnight service on *Savvato tou Pascha.* Naturally since Marigold and I make every effort to integrate into village life, we had duly attended the midnight service before adjourning to Vangelis and Athena's house to join them for the traditional breaking of the Great Lent fast.

We had been delighted when Athena presented us with large bowls of the aforesaid *mayiritsa,* though somewhat less delighted when Vangelis filled us in on the vital ingredients. Not wishing to cause offence by refusing such generous Greek hospitality, it had taken every bit of stubborn resolve to taste the vile smelling soup. Even so, I had struggled to get more than a spoonful down. Marigold flatly refused to even dip her spoon into the thick and murky contents of her bowl.

Fortunately, I was able to come up with an inventive yet plausible excuse for leaving the food untouched, claiming that we were so unaccustomed to eating at such a late hour that if any food passed our lips we would be up all night with a shocking case of indigestion. Luckily, Vangelis felt my concocted pain and cleared the bowls away. Unfortunately, the invented indigestion meant we were forced to forgo the more tempting dishes that followed.

Tuning back into what Panos' was saying, I couldn't believe he was still chuntering on about tripe. It was hard to hide my amusement when after demonstrating such passion for eating soup made from intestines and pancreas, Panos professed that Barry's predilection for eating raw *patsas* was nothing short of disgusting.

"You foreigns eat the strange," Panos declared with a shudder.

Chapter 17

Tickling a Fancy

Even though the traffic in town was light at such an early hour, the roads surrounding the market were the epitome of noisy pandemonium. Pick-ups, some with livestock peering over the sides, battered old vans and cars were double parked, irate and impatient drivers blasting their horns and yelling obscenities through open windows, trying to manoeuvre their vehicles through impassable streets. Panos wasted no time joining in the honking, shouting greetings to other farmers he recognised. Eventually, Panos managed to claim a parking space at the side of the market, telling me it was time to get to work and unload our cargo.

With a sack of *vlita* over one shoulder, I dragged another sack in my wake, trailing behind the laden down Panos to the stall he had booked. Even though Panos assured me that he hadn't gone out of his way to park as far away from his stall as possible, my latent hernia disagreed. A seemingly endless succession of identical trips followed until all of Panos' produce was dumped by his stall. I was most impressed that the basket of loose eggs survived the ninety-minute drive intact over potholes and round hairpin bends, with nary a crack amongst them. Unfortunately, Panos entrusted me to carry the basket from the pick-up to the stall: not all of the eggs survived the little trip I took when my foot slipped in some squashed fruit splattered on the ground. The basket went flying out of my hands, the resultant cracks sounding like thunder to my guilty mind.

"Den peirazei, min klais yia spasmena avga." Assuring me it didn't matter, Panos instructed me not to cry over broken eggs. Picking out the

cracked ones already oozing their yolks, Panos tossed them to the market floor where they joined the trodden mess of slippery squashed fruit. I pondered the possibility that the eggy mess would scramble when the sun was at its hottest, if some bedraggled stray didn't happen along to lick up the mess first. I was somewhat relieved to note that a good three dozen eggs still passed muster in spite of my clumsiness.

With all of our produce unloaded, we set about displaying our wares. All around us other stall holders were equally busy setting out their produce. I noted with interest that we didn't appear to have much direct competition for our crops: to our left, the stall was brimming with aubergines, onions, cucumbers and peppers of every hue, whilst to our right the stall was overflowing with fresh fruit: apples, pears, peaches, watermelons and nectarines.

I cast a suitably disparaging look at my neighbour's nectarines, noting with lofty disapproval the way he hosed down his fruit to give it that morning dew touch, only to feel rather foolish when Panos grappled the hosepipe out of his neighbour's hands to give his own nectarines a good dousing. I suppose on reflection it was not exactly a trick, rather a sensible move to ensure the fruit was presented with optimum freshness.

Producing a set of ancient weighing scales and a handful of flimsy plastic bags, Panos directed me to weigh the potatoes and fill each bag with five kilos worth. Panos then scrawled his prices per kilo on several weather-beaten old pieces of cardboard, propping them up amid the loose salad leaves, the nectarines, the eggs, the tomatoes and the potatoes. As soon as everything was set out in order, Panos fired what appeared to be a rhetorical question my way, "*Thes kafe*?" Without bothering to wait for me to confirm if I wanted coffee or not, he marched off. He was gone in a blur of filthy wellies before I could ask him what I was supposed to do next.

Feeling rather self-conscious, I took my place behind the stall, bristling with nervous anticipation. Standing erect, hands clasped behind my back, I surveyed my immediate kingdom, beginning to feel less on edge as the familiar sights and smells of the market worked their magic. The *agora* is always a favourite outing of mine, whether to do a spot of shopping for fresh produce, or as one of the colourful venues on the popular Greek gastronomic tourist tour that I often lead, otherwise known as 'Walk, Talk and

Taste.' This was my first time experiencing the market from the other side of the stall. At this early hour there were few customers; waiting impatiently, I felt rather like a stage actor waiting for the audience to roll up.

Standing around like a spare part, I cast my eyes over my neighbour's cucumbers, amazed by how many of the luscious green fruits were positively curved in shape, flagrantly defying the EU Cucumber Bending Regulation that dictates only straight cucumbers can be sold by market traders. I know from my own gardening experience that some cucumbers grow with a mind of their own, often ending up as bent as a nine bob note. Personally, I find a bit of curvature does not detract from the taste and I would certainly never consign any bendy cucumbers to the bin. On the other hand, I would not dare to test the law by displaying curved cucumbers in a public place where an overzealous market inspector may confiscate them or worse. I must confess that whilst being up on the regulations, I am not au fait with the penalties for breaching them. Still, I reckoned it was the neighbouring stall holder's head on the chopping block if some pedantic jobsworth happened along.

As I mulled over the sheer lunacy of a law

decreeing the shapes of fruit and vegetables, I couldn't fail to notice that my presence was drawing some curious stares from the neighbouring stall holders. I reflected that whilst I would certainly have stood out as a bit of an out of place odd-bod if I'd turned up attired in my usual smart shirt and tie, my presence still seemed to be attracting attention even though I rather blended in by wearing old slacks, a tee-shirt and wellies. Certain I presented the image of a typical Greek market trader, I couldn't account for the interest I appeared to generate.

A youngish chap ambled by, all bronzed and macho with bulging muscles and a luxuriant black moustache, making what I can only assume was a sniggering comment at my expense to my neighbouring stall holders. My mouth hung open in surprise when he addressed me directly, speaking in English with a broad Brummie accent.

"You've got some cojones wearing that tee-shirt, mate. Body of a Greek god? In your dreams."

I surmised from the resultant sniggers that he had helpfully translated the slogan on my tee-shirt for the benefit of my neighbours. I remained gobsmacked, clueless how the young man had known I was English since I hadn't opened my mouth. At least it threw cold water on Marigold's theory that it was my insistence on pairing sandals and socks that gave away my country of origin. I certainly wished that I'd had the foresight to bring a change of sandals with me. Already the heat was making my feet sweat so much inside the rubber that puddles of water were forming inside my wellies.

Fortunately the youngish chap didn't hang around to fire any more slurs in my direction. Amazingly, his comment prompted the fellow with the bendy cucumbers to walk over and greet me. Proffering a hand, he introduced himself as Socrates. Despite his market garb, I thought his name quite fitting; with his grey hair and sharp appraising eyes he exuded the air of a learned philosopher trapped in the body of a humble farmer. The chap on my other side with the newly hosed nectarines followed suit, introducing himself as Aristotle. Despite his name, he didn't appear to be the philosophical type, being a bit rough and ready, sucking a toothpick between clenched teeth as though poised to pluck it out at any moment and use it as a lethal weapon.

It transpired that both men were market

acquaintances of Panos. Though they hailed from different areas, they were all market regulars, making a living through farming and flogging their fresh produce. Since neither man understood a word of English, I had my work cut out being on top of my Greek language game. It turned out that there wasn't much time for chatting with my new acquaintances as the market soon flooded with customers. Before long the trickle of people became a crowd of Greeks eager to snag a fresh bargain. I delighted in observing the mix of people streaming past; smartly dressed middle-aged women intermingled with black clad widows wheeling their shopping trolleys, mothers with excitable children, and old men.

A tad concerned that no one was stopping to examine my wares, I relaxed when Socrates informed me that the shoppers tended to head indoors first to select their fish and meat, before deciding on their fruit and veg. A woman stopped at my stall, eyeing the price tag on the five kilo bags of potatoes that I had weighed out earlier. Indicating she would take a bag, I accepted her coins with a smile and bid her a good morning. About to wheel the potatoes away, she stopped in her tracks, eyeing me suspiciously.

"Eisai Germanos?" I was not too taken aback when she asked me if I was German; it was a question I was used to hearing.

"Ochi, eimai Anglika," I clarified I was English.

"I Portogalia skotose tous Anglous," she said, throwing her hands up in the gesture of what can you do.

"Ti?" I was at a loss, clueless what she meant by saying the Portuguese killed the English; I know for a fact that the two nations have never waged war.

"Sto podosfairo," the woman said. The penny dropped; she was referring to the UEFA football rather than some imagined war. It seemed many people had little else but football on their minds, the game still dominating television screens.

Panos eventually returned. About time, I thought, by now gasping for the anticipated coffee. Unfortunately the miniscule cup of stone cold, heavily sweetened Greek coffee was like sugared sludge, leaving a vile gritty taste in my mouth. Spotting me wince in disgust, Aristotle offered me some water in a paper cup. It was only as I slurped the warm stagnant liquid that I realised he had topped up the cup from the hosepipe that had been left coiled in direct sunlight. I fervently hoped that I hadn't just swallowed a stomach churning dose of Legionella.

My interest was sparked by what appeared to be a pair of English tourists or ex-pats strolling towards the stall, the gentleman's socks and sandals being a bit of a giveaway to their country of origin, at least according to Marigold's theory. The woman was way too overdressed for a stroll around the market: done up in a low-cut sundress paired with inappropriate heels, she appeared ready to visit some up-market restaurant for a celebratory evening meal. Their sun darkened, rather than pasty skin, led me to surmise they were possibly Greek residents of English extraction. Watching closely as they stopped at Socrates' stall, I noticed they appeared a tad out of their depth, leading me to presume this was perhaps their first market foray.

Many ex-pats limit their shopping expeditions to Lidl, rather than navigate what they perceive as a potentially hazardous shopping arena that may require them to dabble in the Greek language. Doreen and Norman are prime examples of this reluctance to venture out of their comfort zone, fearful of any direct interaction with non-English speakers in case it exposes their limitations of communication. I find this attitude quite bizarre in people who are seemingly adventurous enough to flit to foreign parts in the first place, but it is not uncommon. Doreen attempted to describe this said reluctance as akin to a fear of being let loose in a lion's den, but Marigold is of the opinion that it is Norman who holds his wife back: Norman does have the unfortunate tendency of raising his voice as though that will magically make non-English speaking Greeks understand him, a most unfortunate and embarrassing trait. However, I digress: I will return forthwith to the out of depth ex-pats eyeing up the aubergines on Socrates' stall.

Helpfully holding three fingers up whilst pointing at the aubergines, the unsuitably dressed woman said, "*Tria*" very loudly. Even though she over accentuated the stress accent over the wrong letters, at least I admired her efforts in giving the Greek word a go. As Socrates began piling aubergines into a bag, preparing to weigh out three kilos, the woman began to panic, shouting, "No," in both English and Greek. Tutting in confusion, Socrates tipped the aubergines back out of the bag. A tad flummoxed, the woman repeated her request for three. Socrates shrugged in confusion before once again beginning to fill the bag with aubergines. Realising that the woman wanted just three aubergines, rather than three kilos of the vegetable, I helpfully interceded, telling Socrates, *"Thelei mono treis melitzanes, ochi tria kila."*

It was evident to me from watching the way that Greek people shopped, swooping up huge bags of vegetables, that the stallholders were not accustomed to customers purchasing such meagre quantities as only three aubergines or a single cucumber. Since Greeks are hospitable by nature, they tend to cook a multitude of dishes just on the off-chance that some starving friend or family member may pop round and need feeding up as though they haven't eaten in a week. I have noticed the pitying looks when Vangelis or Spiros drop in unannounced at meal times and I try to gauge how we can prise an additional portion out of a meal designed for two. Apart from my extravagance in always making too much chutney, Marigold and I tend to only cook enough for our needs since we abhor unnecessary waste: then again, I suspect many of my Greek neighbours use any leftovers as animal swill, despite the illegality of this potentially disease spreading insanitary habit. I like to think that my constant lectures on the subject are beginning to make a difference to my neighbours' attitude to swill.

My intervention on the aubergine front drew the enthusiastic attention of the ex-pat woman. Zoning in on me, she flicked her hair in a move that was anything but casual. Sucking her stomach in and thrusting her barely covered bosom out, she explained in a breathy rush of age inappropriate giggles that it was their first visit to the market and she was determined to try out a few of the basic Greek words she had learnt.

"We just moved to Greece two months ago and only started Greek lessons in the last fortnight. It's a bit daunting actually using it; the pronunciation is so difficult, it's not easy to get one's tongue around it." The tip of her tongue darted between pouted lips as she spoke: I can only imagine she mistakenly assumed the gesture was sexy. Without wishing to sound boastful, it appeared that I had inexplicably tickled her fancy.

In all honesty, I cannot say that this type of unwanted female attention is a total novelty since moving to Greece. Occasionally, when I lead a tourist excursion, there may be the odd overeager woman, or desperate as Barry prefers to label them. Married women patently bored of their ever so dull husbands and longing for their very own Shirley Valentine moment, or single or divorced predatory creatures wistfully dreaming of a holiday romance, attempt to attach themselves to me like limpets. I don't flatter myself it is because I am irresistible, but recognise they are lonely and craving attention. Naturally, since I only have eyes for Marigold, I have no interest at all in encouraging any random women whose fancy I may tickle. Fortunately, Sakis is usually along to drive the coach: being younger, better looking and more exotic than me by way of being a handsome moustached Greek, I can usually steer any admirers in his direction, even though he loathes the attention even more than I do. Sakis truly hates the thought of making his girlfriend jealous.

Naturally, if I relay to Marigold any incidences of women making eyes at me, she accuses me of being delusional. It is certainly a phenomenon that has only happened to me since moving to Greece. Even though I encountered many women in restaurant kitchens and dining rooms during my illustrious career as a public health inspector, I never tended to attract any desperate types whilst clad in a neatly pressed white coat and the regulation hairnet that I wore in compliance with hygiene directives.

My reflections were interrupted by Panos nudging me sharply in the side, hissing something along the lines of, "With a bit of encouragement, you could sell this one some *vlita*. Chat her up a bit, Victor." Admittedly his words were a tad cruder in the original Greek.

Considering that a bit of 'chat up' may be a typical market tactic, I decided to play along. I may not be the Del Boy of Meli, but I could be inspired by his gift of the gab. At the very least it would amuse Barry in the recounting.

"Well, the locals certainly appreciate it when we make the effort to speak Greek," I said to the woman, hoping my wellies didn't squelch too much when I moved.

The man that I presumed was the woman's husband lurked behind her looking decidedly uncomfortable. I couldn't help but notice that he appeared to be judging my tee-shirt and finding it lacking, as though anyone vulgar enough to turn out in public in such an appalling item of clothing should be beneath his wife's notice. I supposed his reaction was pretty natural; I would certainly go out of my way to avoid mingling with anyone as tastelessly turned out as I was at that moment, especially as his wife was now batting her eyelashes at me in a shameless attempt to flirt. For all he knew, I could be a disreputable type with shady intentions, trying to lure his wife to my stall with talk of fresh *vlita*. The very thought prompted me to take advantage in the hope of getting rid of a sack of the stuff.

"Perhaps I could tempt you with some fresh *vlita* from my stall," I said to the woman.

"Ooh, that sounds interesting, what is it?" the woman asked with another obvious flick of her hair.

"Salad leaves."

"We haven't started our lessons on fruit and vegetables yet. We're still trying to master animals and colours." Demonstrating her progress in the lessons, the woman announced in the most dreadful Greek accent, *"To kotopoulo einai roz, to kotopoulo einai prasino."* Despite her dire pronunciation, I understood her.

"Well, if you do happen to see any green chickens on the meat stalls inside the market, I'd give them a wide berth. They are probably riddled with salmonella," I advised with a knowing wink.

"Oh, you understood what I said," the woman gushed in delight. "Gosh, we still have such a lot to learn; it may be years until we're fluent enough to come out with difficult words like salmonella."

"It's not difficult at all, the Greek word for salmonella is simply *salmonela,* just remember to stress the e. A personal trick of mine which I use to expand my Greek vocabulary is to make a list of as many words as I can that are almost the same in Greek and English."

"What a brilliant idea. Are there many?" the woman asked, her scarlet painted fingernails stretching out towards my arm.

"Thousands. Just off the top of my head there's *ombrela, banana* and *sokolata,*" I said, edging backwards.

"That's so much more useful to know than green chickens," the woman said with what she likely imagined was a tinkling laugh but actually sounded like a drain being unblocked. "I can count up to ten orange cows, but I still haven't got a clue what day of the week it is."

"If you've quite finished chatting up my wife…" the man stepped forward and intervened.

"Perish the very thought, I have a very attractive wife of my own, I've no need for someone else's seconds. I was merely attempting to be sociable and sell some *vlita,*" I said, drawing myself up to my full height and looking down on him.

Blushing profusely, the woman rushed to say, "Take no notice of Andy; he's gone and got himself all overheated, it makes him short-tempered. Andy, apologise at once."

"I didn't realise you were English, I couldn't hear you talking over all this din," Andy mumbled by way of apology. "You'd be short tempered too if you were dragged round a market in this heat."

And forced to watch while your wife flirts right under your nose, I thought. In truth I could sympathise: though not quite as obvious, Marigold does have a tendency to blush and become rather giddy and girlish around Giannis, the handsome bee man, and around Lefteris, the tattooed leather clad young man with the pampered pet poodle, Fufu. Even though my wife is likely past it in their eyes, they still flatter her with their practiced Greek charm.

"It takes a while to acclimatise to the change in temperature," I said, grabbing the hosepipe and directing it towards them. "A quick burst with this will soon cool you down."

Taking his wife firmly by the arm, Andy dragged his wife away before I could drench the pair of them.

"Flertarei mazi sou, Victor," Panos chortled, saying she had been flirting with me.

"To xero," I replied, acknowledging that it was true. Perhaps my inappropriate tee-shirt gave me a bad-boy image that appealed.

"Tin epomeni for a pou mia koritsi flertarei mazi sou, pouliste tis merikes patates," Panos laughed, telling me that the next time a woman flirted with me to at least sell her some potatoes.

Panos had a fair point. I'd let the ex-pats slip through my hands without selling them anything. I made a mental note to watch a few more episodes of 'Only Fools and Horses' if Panos demanded that I accompany him to market again: I could do with picking up a few tips from Del Boy. Smiling to myself, I wondered if lovely jubbly was translatable.

Chapter 18

The Del Boy of Meli

We were soon so swamped with customers that I wondered how Panos possibly managed without me on his usual market trips. Between weighing out the produce, interacting with the hordes descending on our choice fresh selection, and sorting out change, it was most definitely a two-person job. Amidst the general bustle, I had to admit I was in my element, though my enjoyment was somewhat tempered by the constant chaffing of soggy socks inside my wellies and the odd smirk cast in my direction from English-reading Greeks when they clocked the rather inapt slogan on my by now sweaty tee-shirt.

As the morning wore on in a seemingly endless fashion, I began to ache from the constant bending down to haul five kilo bags of potatoes. It could certainly be classed as the type of manual labour I was unaccustomed to. Towards noon, the crowd of market goers began to thin out and I took a well-deserved breather. Declining the offer of a tipple of *tsipouro* from Aristotle's hip flask, I sated my thirst with a juicy nectarine while Panos puffed away on a cigarette.

Keen to hear Panos' opinion on the EU Cucumber Bending Regulation, I asked him what his thoughts were on the matter.

"Ti pisteveta yia ton kanonismo kampsis angouriou?"

"Ti?" Panos responded with a confused, "What?"

"To schima tou angouriou," I said, clarifying that I was referring to the law proscribing the shape of cucumbers.

"Prepei na einai asteio, den to echo akousei pote." Panos insisted it must be a joke, he had never heard of it.

"Kanena asteio, einai alithea." I assured Panos it was no joke, it was true.

Throwing his head back in the typical Greek nod of disbelief and clucking his tongue, Panos shouted to Socrates and Aristotle, something along the lines of my being addled in the head, telling them I had fallen for some nonsense about laws dictating the shape of cucumbers.

Whilst Aristotle almost choked on his *tsipouro,* Socrates doubled over with laughter, spluttering, *"Ypotheto oti echoun kai nomo yia tis bananes."* Mentally translating his words, I worked out that he had said he supposed there was a law for bananas too. His sarcasm was hard to miss.

"O nomos yia tis bananes einai mythos," I replied, confirming the banana law was a myth. Unable to come up with the necessary Greek vocabulary on the spur of the moment to explain that the English press continued to insist the EU banana myth was reality, I let the matter drop.

I reflected that many of the European Union regulations which the British allowed themselves to be subjected to with collective moaning, were simply disregarded within Greece. I recollected Nikos' reluctance to abide by the law banning pig swill and I couldn't remember the last time I had seen a Greek or Albanian builder's head encased in a protective hard hat, even when they were wobbling atop precarious scaffolding. Dina never once put out a cautionary yellow plastic sign warning of the hazards of a freshly mopped floor, though admittedly the taverna floor rarely got a good mopping, and all the 'No Smoking' signs were placed above conveniently placed ashtrays. Whilst the British knuckled down in the manner of compliant law-abiding citizens, the Greeks were defiant to the point of not even knowing that half of the laws which they flouted existed in the first place.

Whilst I mulled over the marked differences between my native and adopted nations, Panos, Socrates and Aristotle took advantage of the lull between customers to engage in a noisy and fast-paced political argument. Their heated discussion was punctuated with dramatic gestures and the odd expletive which Barry would be better placed than myself to translate. It seemed that Panos, being a life-long supporter of the reigning *Nea Dimokratia,* had little time for Aristotle's communist leanings. Unable to keep up with their back and forth altercation, I tuned out, reflecting that I really ought to put more effort into perfecting my political Greek since so many heated conversations revolved around the subject. Still, I conjectured, even if I had all the necessary polemic language down pat, I might still fall short unless I brushed up on all the nuances of the various Greek political parties. My knowledge on the matter is at best a tad superficial.

Tuning back in, I noticed that the three way altercation had moved on from politics to philosophy. It amused me to think that if Panos had been named Plato rather than Panayiotis, then nothing much would have changed in Greece over the last two plus centuries as the modern threesome continued the noble tradition of Greek philosophers arguing in the market place. Of course my analogy was a tad off since the original Aristotle had not been a contemporary of the learned philosophical pair.

Remembering Barry's request that I pick up some honeycomb tripe, I slipped away and headed towards the indoor market where the butchers' shops, known as *kreatagora,* were located. After standing outside in the heat for so long, I found the smell of meaty flesh and the sight of butchered carcasses suspended from hooks a tad nauseating. A burly butcher outfitted in a bloodied white coat and wielding a blood stained cleaver, did nothing to quell my biliousness. Raising his eyebrows in wry amusement as he clocked the slogan on my tee-shirt, he retrieved a dog end from behind one ear. I hurried past before he could strike a match. Even if he happened to have the tastiest cow's stomachs in Greece, nothing would induce to me to make a purchase from such an unhygienic fellow.

Relaying my request for *patsas* to the next butcher along, I was not in the least tempted by his attempts to sell me some pig intestines or a lamb's head. I tried to describe the appearance of honeycomb tripe, eventually pulling out my handy pocket dictionary and asking for *kirithra,* honeycomb. I wasn't too surprised when the obliging chap gave me directions to a nearby stall selling local honey. Approaching a third *kreatagora* without much optimism that I would be able to satisfy Barry's desire for tripe, I was delighted when the butcher announced he did have *patsas kirithra.* The greyish mass he produced with a flourish resembled a rancid old towel that had been used to clean the drains. Funnily enough, it bore a similar smell.

"Einai to kalytero stomachi provatou," he

announced, declaring it was the best sheep's stomach. *"Poly kalo sti soupa me ta podia,"* he beamed, telling me it was very good in soup with feet. I was in two minds what to do. The tripe didn't look anything like the honeycomb stuff that Barry had requested, nor did it come from a cow, but it may well hold a certain nostalgic appeal for my brother-in-law.

My mind flashed back to an incident several decades earlier when Barry had been a newlywed, the first time around. One warm summer evening, Barry's first wife Kimberly, invited Marigold and I round for a meal. Desperate to make a good impression on her new in-laws, Kimberly pulled out all the salad stops, opening a tin of salmon and splashing out on a new bottle of Heinz salad cream. Barry was late getting home, leaving Kimberly to entertain us in his absence, all the while visibly fretting over the wilting lettuce whilst trying to get on Marigold's good side. Kimberly's sycophantic efforts were painfully obvious, leaving Marigold cold. My wife has never had much time for social climbers and never really took to Kimberly.

Barry was full of apologies when he finally arrived, our presence apparently a complete surprise. Never one for eating anything green back in the day, Barry took one look at the salad and exclaimed that it was a good job he'd stopped to pick up a nice piece of tripe. Rifling through the cupboards for a bottle of malt vinegar, he complained that rabbit food was hardly suitable sustenance after a hard day's graft. He announced that he would just pop out for a bag of chips to go with the lovely piece of honeycomb.

Clearly mortified by her husband's preference for such peasant fare, Kimberly roasted Barry, screeching that he was deliberately trying to show her up by going out of his way to be common. Raking Barry over the coals in front of his precious and over-protective sister was not the wisest of moves, especially when Kimberly banned Barry from darkening their door with tripe ever again. Despite Marigold's personal opinion that tripe was repugnant, she leapt to Barry's defence, bristling at the very idea that her brother might be considered common. After that, whenever Barry and Kimberly were embroiled in a domestic, Marigold made a point of welcoming Barry to ours with open arms, always ensuring that there was a nice plate of tripe and raw onions waiting for him. Whilst Marigold is not one to generally hold a grudge, her grudge against Kimberly outlasted Barry's first marriage. To this day, she still refers to her ex sister-in-law as 'that dreadful woman who thought tinned salmon was posh.'

"*Theleis afto to stomachi apo ta provata*?" The butcher asking if I wanted the sheep stomach brought me back to the present.

"*Nai, kai rixte sta podia.*" Yes, I said, telling him to throw in the feet. If Barry had no use for my purchase, I could always palm it off on Panos, to feed to his dog. By taking a bite out of Guzim's bottom, the filthy mutt had demonstrated it clearly wasn't fussy what it ate.

After snapping up a bar of pistachio *halva* as a treat for Marigold, I returned to Panos' stall, asking the welly wearing farmer if he'd managed without my help. I was a tad put out when Panos told me that in truth I had been more of a hindrance than a help, what with dropping the eggs and selling the choicest nectarines he'd stashed at the back before any of the mankier ones he had strategically placed up front.

"*Kapoios tha piveste oti den echete doulepsei pote se mia agora,*" Panos declared.

"*Alla den to echo.*" Panos' statement that anyone would think that I had never worked on a market before was only worthy of the honest reply, "But I haven't." I really don't know where Panos got the ridiculous notion that I was a bit of a Del Boy.

With Panos grumbling in Greek, I tuned out, my attention riveted on a group of four English people approaching the stall. I recognised one of them as an ex-pat who lived on the coast, his considerable bulk making him hard to forget. His name was on the tip of my tongue: *Terastios*. Spotting me, he made his way over, greeting me by name. Fortunately, I had a sudden recollection that *Terastios* was only the nickname the Greeks gave him because they couldn't get their tongues around his actual name of Hugh, the Greek moniker being the translation of huge.

The rather anorexic looking woman holding onto Hugh's arm had clearly fallen for the spell of the market, declaring it was quite wonderful.

"You've missed the best of it, most of the stall holders are beginning to pack up for the day," I informed her.

"We'd have been here earlier, but it was impossible to park," Hugh explained. "We've been driving round in circles for hours. The car park was jammed solid and when we finally found a space we couldn't work out if we needed a ticket; all the signs were in Greek and we didn't fancy risking the wrath of a traffic warden."

I bit my tongue. Whilst it was patently absurd to turn up at the market mid-morning when the parking situation would be deplorable, rather than first thing, I had to sympathise with Hugh's natural reluctance to get on the wrong side of the law.

"I do hope we're not too late to pick up some fresh salad stuff," his wife said. "Hugh is on strict orders that it's nothing but salads for the foreseeable, the doctor has recommended he goes on a strict diet on account of his blood pressure. He's in danger of exploding if he doesn't shift some weight."

Rather like Violet Burke's feet, I thought to myself.

"Well, you won't find fresher *vlita* than this anywhere. It was still pushing up soil at dawn," I said, using a little white lie to exaggerate its freshness. In truth, the *vlita* was looking remarkably spruce, having just benefited from a hosing down.

"*Vlita*, never heard of it," Hugh said emphatically.

"Seriously, how can you live in Greece and

not be familiar with the tastiest, most exquisite, salad leaves?" I said, feigning shock. I have to say I did a pretty good job of sounding sincere considering I'd never heard of the stuff myself until the day before.

With Panos' words about my uselessness still ringing in my ears, I launched into a persuasive sales spiel on the merits of *vlita,* assuring my now captive audience of Hugh, his wife and their two companions that *vlita* is one of the most remarkable foods for dieters, well known for its miraculous ability to satiate the stomach whilst staving off hunger. I must give full credit to Douglas for filling me in all the weight watching jargon during our experimental forays in the kitchen. Additionally, since Panos had deliberately misled me into believing that I would be picking the stuff, I had taken the precaution of leafing through Marigold's collection of cookery books and could now reel off a delicious Greek recipe that would tempt even a committed carnivore.

"No Greek table would be complete without a luscious green dish of *vlita,* or amaranth salad, dressed with a squeeze of lemon and a drizzle of extra virgin," I said with heartfelt conviction. Even though the market shoppers had begun to thin out, my passionate speech was beginning to attract a wide audience, with a couple of Greek-Canadians translating my English words to interested passersby stopping to stare at the show. "Amaranth salad is not just a delight for the eyes and the taste buds; it is packed with vitamins, fibre and protein. No doubt you are up to date with the latest acclaimed superfoods with their health giving properties..."

"Like goji berries; they're the height of culinary fashion," the Greek-Canadian woman enthused.

"Well, you can forget all about your goji berries and chia seeds, amaranth leaves are about to be recognised as the hottest, must-have superfood. Since the secret isn't quite out there yet, you can still snap them up without paying the hefty price the leaves will command when word gets out..."

"Victor knows what he's on about," Hugh said, a serious expression plastered on his face. "He was big in something to do with food back in the UK."

I didn't bother to disillusion him by revealing that I had been big in food hygiene, rather than food nutrition or gastronomic trends.

"Well, if it's an undiscovered fashionable

superfood, we must buy it up, there may well be a shortage when word gets out," the Greek-Canadian proclaimed, seemingly unaware of the irony that their eagerness to bulk buy might lead to shortages.

Panos gawped in amazement as a veritable crowd descended on the stall like a pack of locusts, practically fighting each other to buy up the *vlita*. The two English couples, along with the Greek-Canadians, negotiated the price of a sack full, having absorbed the information I had imparted on how the leaves shrink to a quarter of their size during the simmering process.

"I never before to see the people to fight over the *vlita*, the world is gone the mad," an astonished Panos said in his native tongue. "Victor, what is the superfood you to talk of?"

"Something gullible people fall for," I told him. Basking in Panos' stated opinion that I was not so useless after all, I accepted a well-earned tipple of tsipouro from Aristotle's hip-flask.

Chapter 19

Insincere Flattery

There was no sign of Marigold back at the house, though the Punto was parked outside. I received a warm welcome home from Pickles, playfully nipping at my ankles: considering the state of my socks, I am of the opinion the kitten has lost all sense of smell. Even though I could see through his subterfuge, the kitten's affection likely faked to win himself a treat of sardines, I headed into the kitchen and opened a tin, glad there was no one around to notice what a sucker I am. There was a note from Marigold informing me that she was popping over to Athena's house. Presuming she was having her hair done prior to Apostolos' name day party, I made a mental note to make a fuss of her hair on her return. I knew from experience that failing to notice when she'd had her hair done would guarantee me a place in the marital doghouse.

The first order of business was a refreshing shower to wash away the manly smell of my manual labours. Unfortunately, my earlier fear that the tank may be running on dry was confirmed when nothing came out of the taps. Thwarted in my wish to get clean, I focused instead on my rumbling stomach: I hadn't eaten anything since breakfast at Panos' house. Full of praise for the inspired way I had sold every last *vlita* leaf from the market stall, Panos had promised me a slap-up lunch. Unfortunately, Panos' idea of slap-up and mine were not quite the same. Earlier, I felt my stomach sink when he parked up on the seafront outside the fast food chain, Goody's Burger House. Recalling the Goody's bags littering his tractor, I surmised that Panos was a bit of a fast-food junkie. The thought of inhaling the greasy aroma of burgers and chips on the long drive back home turned my stomach, but Panos announced we would eat inside as he didn't want fast food cartons littering the interior of his pristine pick-up. Despite my reservations that by now we looked like a pair of welly wearing sweaty reprobates, the welcoming staff made no attempt to sling us out.

"Ela, Victor, o, ti thelis." Panos' generous gesture inviting me to have whatever I wanted left me cold. Without wishing to sound snobbish, I have never indulged in fast food. Although the chain restaurant appeared to be scrupulously clean, I have always made a point of avoiding mass produced hamburgers and chicken nuggets, being too familiar for comfort with the sort of pink slime that is pumped into them. In my experience, there would likely be more parts of intestine and feet, not to mention cartilage scrapings and a sludge of random droppings from the abattoir floor, to be found in factory made fast food offerings than there were in the *kreatagoras* on the market.

Panos placed his order for a bacon and cheese hamburger with fries, whilst I opted for a glass of carrot juice, telling Panos that I was saving my appetite for the party later. Less than convinced, Panos pointed towards the salad bar, saying, *"Yparchei i salata bar."* Admittedly, the array of fresh salads looked tasty, but nothing would tempt me to indulge. Pre-prepared salads are a risk too far: they could turn into an unhygienic nightmare if temperatures are less than optimally maintained. It would only take one customer to cough or sneeze over the salad selection to start a chain reaction of disgusting bacterial growth. Still, in fairness, the paper cup of carrot juice was excellent. Not only was it most refreshing, but I'd hazard a guess it contained a smattering of an actual carrot.

I decided to enjoy a late lunch before traipsing out to the village tap to fill up the water bottles. Marigold would not be best pleased to discover she would need to wash in a bucket prior to the party. Eyeing Pickles' bowl of food, I thought a quick snack of sardines on toast would be just the ticket. Alas, the cat already had its face submerged in the contents of the very last tin, dribbling over the oily fish. Although I was quite tempted to throw a Fray Bentos in the oven, my stomach objected to waiting for the pastry to puff up inside the tin. Instead, I was pleased to discover a tub of homemade *tzatziki* in the fridge that passed the sniff test.

Deciding it would go nicely with some freshly fried *saganaki* and a handful of juicy black Kalamata olives, I set to cutting a thick slice of *kefalotyri* cheese and dousing it in flour.

Finally sated on *saganaki* and *tzatziki,* I pondered what to do with the remainder of my free afternoon. Reflecting that the blissful peace of the moment would fly out of the window when my mother arrived the next day, I made a mental note to badger Barry into making an early start on the *apothiki*. There would be much more chance of peace and quiet once Violet Burke was installed out of the way in the downstairs storage. I would turn my persuasive charm on later when I popped round to deliver Barry's bag of tripe.

Deciding this may be a good opportunity to pen another chapter of the sequel to my still-stuffed-in-the-drawer moving abroad book, I tried to recall exactly where I had left events. I smiled to myself, remembering that Vangelis had just discovered a job lot of Burnt Sunshine paint and the pair of us were about to give the filthy, smoke-blackened taverna ceiling a facelift. The bright orange paint we had slapped on was already beginning to fade away beneath a new layer of soot and mosquito infested cobwebs. There was little chance of us repeating our charitable efforts since Nikos hadn't even noticed the fruit of our labours the first time around.

Grabbing a notepad, I adjourned to the balcony to pen some more of my memories about our first winter in Meli. Flicking through the pages, I realised I had accidentally picked up a notepad full of Marigold's scribblings, the exclamation mark strewn prose being a bit of a giveaway. At first glance it appeared to be some kind of journal jottings or diary entries. Tempted though I was to read on, it struck me that to do so would be a blatant breach of marital trust that I could not in all conscience countenance. Hurriedly closing the notebook, I returned it to where I had found it, wondering why Marigold had never mentioned to me what she was up to. It briefly crossed my mind that she might be penning a book of her own based on our moving abroad experiences, but I dismissed the notion as too absurd. No one with such scant respect for the correct usage of exclamation marks could be so deluded. I blame Marigold's appalling exclamation habit on her over indulgence of moving abroad books: the amount she has voraciously devoured over the years has clearly played havoc with her ability to spot if something is worthy of exclamation.

Whilst I could somewhat understand Marigold's fascination with the genre when we lived back in Manchester, I find it a tad odd that she is still addicted to reading about other people's up-stick exploits now that we have made our own move abroad. Really, it is quite amazing how some people could imagine their humdrum lives to be so exciting that they bother to pen their experiences. Then again, the great reading public may cast the same scathing judgement over my musings: it is no wonder that my first completed book is still safely stashed away in a drawer, unlikely ever to see daylight.

One moment, I was relaxing on the balcony with my thoughts, the next moment I woke with a terrible crick in my neck. Unused to indulging in the Greek habit of taking a siesta, it took me a minute to get my bearings. I suppose that my unplanned nap could be blamed on Panos dragging me from my bed at such an unearthly hour of the morning.

"Oh, there you are, Victor. What on earth are doing wearing that joke of a tee-shirt? Do tell me you didn't go out in public in it," Marigold chided. "Really, if you are going to siesta you could at least lie down in the bedroom rather than exposing any passersby to the sight of you sprawled around with your mouth gaping open."

My wife made a fair point: wiping away some drool that had caked on my chin, I considered it was hardly dignified to snooze on the balcony. Recalling that Marigold had been in Athena's kitchen, I immediately flattered her with some rather insincere praise about how lovely her hair was looking. In truth, it looked perfectly dreadful, her usual Titian locks appearing lank and greasy.

"Sometimes I despair of you, Victor. Do you ever actually notice my hair or is this just your feeble attempt to be droll? My hair is a total fright because I wasn't able to wash it today. There wasn't a drop of water when I got up this morning, the tank was dry."

"Is the water back yet?" I asked, remembering that I would need to get busy filling bottles if the supply was still off.

"Yes, thank goodness, it came back when I was with Athena."

"Not having your hair done…"

"I went over to discuss the arrangements for

Anastasia's baptism. We decided to have the celebrations at the taverna, rather than at Athena's house. Nikos doesn't open at lunchtime so there won't be any randoms dropping in without an invitation. Nikos says he will rig up that sheet again, the one he used as a sunshade at Barry's wedding."

"Ah, the infamous canapé," I laughed.

"Athena talked Nikos into doing *ourounopoulo* since it's such a special occasion."

"Roast suckling pig. That should go down well if there's plenty of crackling," I said approvingly. "You should knock up one of your trifles, dear. Panos comes over all poetic at the very mention."

"I suppose I could make the effort considering he might end up being your father-in-law," Marigold decided. "Now, what did Panos have to say about his intentions towards your mother? Do tell. I can feel it in my guts that he's infatuated."

"I'm afraid he wasn't very forthcoming. It turns out he's not one for talking about his feelings."

"Oh, you can be so useless, Victor. I suppose you went full foot-in-mouth and blurted it out, rather than attempting to extract the information with a bit of subtlety," Marigold called over her shoulder as she opened the fridge. Scrunching her face up in horror, she exclaimed, "Good grief, it smells as though something has died in here. Do you suppose the septic tank needs emptying?"

"It's probably just the tripe that I picked up for Barry at the market," I clarified.

"Well, you'll have to get rid of it; the smell is beyond rank."

"That's probably the feet," I admitted, taking a certain delight in watching Marigold squirm.

Chapter 20

What Did Socrates Know, Anyway?

"If you're schlepping that rancid bag of innards over to Barry, can you take over some cuttings that I promised Cynthia?" Marigold asked.

"Rightio, let me just jump in the shower first. My muscles are screaming from all the heavy lifting I did at the market…"

"Oh, how you do exaggerate, Victor. I expect you've been sitting around all day chewing the fat with Panos," Marigold said dismissively.

"In between running around after tripe for your brother and searching out your favourite sugary treat," I retorted, presenting my wife with the pistachio *halva* I had bought earlier.

"Oh, you are good to me, darling, you know how much I love *halva*. I'll make a start on the cuttings whilst you jump in the shower. But don't be too long over at Barry's, Sherry will be here soon. Remember, she's tagging along with us to the party."

I groaned aloud at the reminder, muttering under my breath, "I was never very partial to gooseberries." I really wasn't in the mood to be subjected to Sherry's jolly-hockey-sticks patronising manner, or for any of the matchmaking machinations that Marigold had up her sleeve.

The sight of water spouting from the shower nozzle was an immense relief. Soaping up, I looked forward to inviting Violet Burke to partake in my outdoor spa, providing she agreed to wear a swimming costume in the bath. It wouldn't do if a lack of water deprived her of the unique experience, one that would certainly save me worrying if her swollen feet had been submerged in my washing up bowl. The last time my mother visited, I ended up splashing out on Tina's entire stock of washing up bowls, never certain if Vi's feet had been in the latest one whilst my back was turned. No matter how thoroughly I scoured them, I just couldn't take the chance.

The shower worked wonders on my aching muscles; I felt like a new man once my ablutions were complete. Kicking the discarded 'Body of a Greek God' tee-shirt to one side, I decided I may as well gift it to Guzim since I would never be caught dead in the thing again. Better to let Guzim, rather than me, be the butt of juvenile jokes. On reflection, I considered that in comparison to the puny Albanian shed dweller, my body could be described as Greek god-like, well, at a pinch. Perhaps a pinch is a tad delusional; a smidgen might be more apt.

After dressing in a smart button down shirt and tie in readiness for the party, I grabbed the putrid smelling bag of sheep's stomach to deliver to Barry and strode down the outdoor stone stairs. Marigold was a blur amid the riot of vibrant colour at the bottom of the garden where we had planted some vivid purple, red and pink oleanders, hoping to train them up to disguise the intrusive sight of Guzim's fence. Their speed of growth was truly remarkable, their prolific blooms quite dazzling in their beauty.

"Darling, how many times must I tell you not to handle the oleanders without wearing gardening gloves? They are incredibly toxic," I warned my wife for the umpteenth time.

"I'm just taking some cuttings for you to take round to Cynthia. You know how she likes a splash of colour round the ecological pond," Marigold said.

"I'm not sure that the oleanders are a good choice, not with Anastasia about. It won't be long until she has her fingers into everything and these plants are incredibly poisonous," I said.

"You and your poison obsession," Marigold scoffed. "I'm sure if you had your way we would all be wrapped up in plastic to avoid touching anything potentially lethal."

"I think you are being a tad dramatic. Did you see me stripping our walls back in Manchester after I read that fascinating theory that Napoleon was poisoned by toxic wallpaper?" I asked rhetorically. "Of course not, it was likely an arsenic fluke. Still, there's no point in deliberately ignoring toxic threats that are directly under our noses."

"Are you sure the oleanders pose a risk, or

are you simply hyperbolising?" Marigold asked, doubt beginning to creep into her voice.

"I am positive; oleanders contain dangerous levels of toxins. Only recently, I read about a case in America where a man was accused of murdering a rival mortician by spiking his drink with oleander: the case was only dropped because it was too difficult for the prosecution to prove that traces of toxic oleandrin were present in the corpse."

"Now you mention it, I do recall there was something similar…what was it?" Marigold questioned, her brow furrowed in concentration. "Oh, I know, that mousy woman…what was her name? Edna Pearson, that was it, it's coming back to me now. She worked in the prison kitchen until word got out that she poisoned her husband with oleander tea…now I think on it, she definitely tried to do him in with the plant. It didn't actually kill him, but it made him dreadfully sick and landed her with a stretch inside."

"I don't remember reading about that," I said in surprise. Marigold rarely pays much attention to the news. "Where was it?"

"Australia, dear. It was on 'Prisoner: Cell Block H.'"

"That dreadful Australian soap opera with the wobbly sets? What on earth were you doing watching such drivel?"

"That's beside the point," Marigold said, blushing scarlet as she realised she had outed herself as a secret fan of the prison soap, despite repeatedly denying it. "The point is that they ran a storyline about the toxicity of oleanders…thus demonstrating that you are correct. Best not to take any over to Cynthia, it's too much of a risk to have them near the baby. Perhaps we should get rid of ours, just to be on the safe side."

"Let's reassess the situation once Anastasia is actually toddling…"

I didn't have chance to finish my sentence before Marigold interrupted, steamrolling in. "If we dig up the poisonous oleanders we could replace them with whatever it is that releases that intoxicating scent we can smell after sunset, it's just heavenly."

"I believe you are referring to Angel's Trumpets," I said. Once it was dark the heady aroma wafted through Meli, permeating the air. Marigold had described the sweet and powerful scent to a tee. It was indeed intoxicating, perhaps not surprising as the plant is a known hallucinogenic.

"Is that the one with the white pendulous bell flowers?" Marigold queried.

"That's the one. It seems a bit pointless to dig up the oleanders though, only to replace them with something equally poisonous."

"Victor, really. You appear obsessed with seeing danger lurking in nature."

"Not at all, dear. I am simply stating the facts. Even the humble daffodil can be dangerous..."

"It's a pity no one bothered to tell Wordsworth. When he was wandering as lonely as a cloud and happened upon a field of daffs, he wrote, 'A poet could not but be gay, in such a jocund company.' If he'd listened to you, the field would have been sprawled with dead bodies rather than gay poets," Marigold said with a rather dramatic eye roll. A tad taken aback to hear my wife quoting one of the Lake Poets, I recalled her telling me she had been forced to memorise Wordsworth back in her school days. Clearly her comprehension skills were a tad lacking when it came to interpreting poetry.

"Well, since we are in Greece, you may be interested to hear that Socrates referred to daffodils as 'the chaplet of the infernal gods,' because of the toxic lycorine found in their bulbs. If one ingests lycorine it can lead to nausea, vomiting and diarrhoea..."

"I'm hardly likely to go round snacking on daffodils. Anyway, it strikes me as a bit lame for you to cite Socrates as an authority on poison. What did he know after all? I suppose you think he was just having an off day when he drank that lethal cup of hemlock. He didn't see that one coming, did he?"

"Well, actually he did..." I began to say, but thought better of it. Marigold would hardly be interested in all the grisly details of the noble philosopher's last moments. Instead, I pointed out, "Hemlock. Another dangerous plant that grows wild in the local olive groves."

"Perhaps we should just have the garden cemented over to be on the safe side," Marigold said with a hefty drip of sarcasm.

"All this, simply because I reminded you to wear your gardening gloves," I harrumphed. From the corner of my eye I spotted Guzim sidling through the gap in the fence, a hangdog expression plastered on his face, no doubt after the sympathy vote. I was in no mood to be cornered.

"Perhaps concreting the garden isn't such a

bad idea, at least it would give me a good excuse to sack Guzim," I fired at Marigold as a parting shot before stomping off to Barry's.

"Jeepers creepers. What have you got in that bag, Victor? It smells like something has crawled out of the drains." Barry recoiled in disgust as I collided with him in the village square.

"It's your tripe, I was just bringing it over to yours," I replied.

"Well, don't bother. There's no amount of malt vinegar could drown out that stench. Just toss it in the nearest bin."

"That's gratitude for you. I trawled the length and breadth of the market to get my hands on this."

"Sorry, Victor, I know you meant well," Barry apologised. "I'm just a bit out of sorts as Athena has just summoned me: again. It's been one thing after another with that dratted woman all week. I don't know why she said she would take charge of the baptism when she insists on consulting me about every little detail."

"I expect she just doesn't want you to feel left out," I said, adding, "Marigold's going to do one of her trifles."

"Ah well, that makes up for a lot, you can't

beat one of my sis's trifles. I'd best be getting over there and see what Athena wants this time."

"Will you be joining us at Apostolos' name day party later?" I asked.

"Only if he doesn't expect me to start frequenting his barber's shop. I'm not keen on the local look of a lopsided neckline," Barry laughed, tempting me to remind him of his infamous mullet. "Go on, I'll try and persuade Cyn to put her glad rags on; a night out will do her good."

"Excellent," I remarked, gleefully swinging the bag of tripe as I turned about face to head home. I am certainly blessed in my brother-in-law; Barry invariably has the knack of lightening my mood, no matter how foul.

Chapter 21

Greek Expectations

"Your hair really does look lovely," I complimented my wife. Watching her tease her damp Titian locks into place, my flattering remark was genuine this time. Marigold's eyes met mine in the mirror; we shared a smile, our earlier spat forgotten.

"Gosh, it completely slipped my mind, Victor. We need to take some kind of gift along for Apostolos. We can't possibly turn up empty-handed to his name day celebration."

"I rather thought that the person celebrating their name day was supposed to hand out cakes or chocolate to those wishing them *Xronia Polla,*" I said falteringly, a tad uncertain of Greek expectations surrounding name day customs.

"I don't think we should risk it, Victor. It wouldn't look good if we are the only ones arriving not bearing gifts," Marigold argued. "It's a pity that you wore that tee-shirt today and made it all sweaty, otherwise we could have re-gifted it to Apostolos. He always strikes me as a chap with a sense of humour."

"That would account for his neckline cuts. I'm going to give the tee-shirt to Guzim; you know how he's always badgering me for my castoffs."

"That's because he can appreciate style when he sees it," Marigold said, almost choking with laughter. "And because his wife in Albania eats all his money."

"Very droll, dear. It still leaves us in a bit of a pickle over what to gift Apostolos."

"If you think for one minute that I'm going to let you hand over the kitten…"

"I didn't say Pickles, I said we were in a pickle," I pointed out. How Marigold could imagine for one moment that I would ever give the kitten away to a man who wielded a lopsided razor for a living was quite beyond me. I had grown rather fond of Pickles, despite him being the spawn of Kouneli, Cynthia's vile rapist tomcat.

"You were eager enough to get rid of Tesco," Marigold accused.

"Tesco was an excellent emotional support animal to Leo, and you know how Sampaguita dotes on it."

"She'll be back tomorrow. I'm so looking forward to seeing her again, she's like a breath of fresh air," Marigold gushed.

"It will certainly be good to see Spiros with a smile on his face again. The poor chap has been pining for her return."

"You could always give that chicken of yours to Apostolos; you know the one with the gammy leg."

"I am very attached to Raki. It's not going anywhere," I said, closing the subject down. Marigold appeared somewhat obsessed with getting rid of Raki, though admittedly her latest gem that we gift it to Apostolos was a tad less drastic than her suggestion of throwing it in the pot with potatoes and garlic.

"We'll just take Apostolos a bottle of Lidl

red and be done with it."

"Whatever you think is best, dear. Now, do go and dispose of that smelly tee-shirt whilst I decide what to wear."

"Don't take too long about it. Sherry could be here any moment and I don't want lumbering with the ghastly woman," I said, scooping up the tee-shirt I'd worn to the market, along with the mud smeared pyjama bottoms, and heading outside to find Guzim.

I caught up with Guzim in the garden, hosing the vegetable patch down with a desultory air about him.

"Pos einai to kefali sou simera?" I said, asking him how his head was today, imagining him to be suffering a horrendous hangover after imbibing so much medicinal *ouzo*.

Guzim stared at me as though I was simple, before throwing his head back and clucking his tongue as though he was an actual Greek.

"O skylos dankose to kato meros, ochi to kefali mou." Guzim informed me that the dog bit his bottom, not his head.

"To xero. Pos einai o gloutos sou?" I told him I knew that, before asking him how his buttock was.

"Nomizo oti einai ligo prosopiko," Guzim practically spat at me. I struggled to contain my mirth at his outrage. Really, the very notion that Guzim would tell me my question was a bit personal after he'd been flashing far more of his bottom in my face than any buttock shy onlooker should be forced to endure struck me as patently ludicrous.

"Douleves simera i isastan arrostos?" I asked Guzim if he'd worked today or if he'd been sick.

"Imoun arrostos alla doulevo. Tha prepei na." Guzim informed me he was sick but he worked, he had to. I suppressed a snort, all too familiar with the inevitable line that would follow. I would wager good money on him telling me that his wife in Albania ate all his money. Bang on the nail, Guzim predictably announced, *"I ynaika stin Alvania troei ola ta chrimata."*

"Den peirazei, echo ena doro yia sena." Guzim dropped his dejected stance, flashing me a toothless smile when I told him that I had a present for him. Amazingly, the smile didn't drop when he saw the sweat stained tee-shirt bearing the slogan 'Body of a Greek God.' Staring at the words, he asked me to translate.

Guzim's hearty response of, *"Kalo, kalo, ego to soma etsi,"* took me somewhat by surprise. I had hardly expected him to declare it was good because he had a body like that. Perchance, I had mis-translated the slogan and told him that the tee-shirt said 'puny, toothless and shabby'. Not even in his wildest dreams could Guzim be so delusional as to think his scrawny body bore any resemblance to that of a Greek god. I was even more flummoxed when Guzim announced that he would wear it to the party. Perhaps there was some Albanian shindig going down in the area. I couldn't imagine that the toothless shed dweller had managed to wheedle himself an invitation to the same select gathering that we were attending.

Remembering that I had scooped up the muddy pyjama bottoms that I had been wearing during my recent frog encounter, I told Guzim that I had some trousers for him too, "*Echo ki ego panteloni.*" I will confess to feeling a tad guilty when he swooped on them in delight, telling me he couldn't work out what had happened to the ugly trousers that I had given him the day before. I had no intention of telling him that I had stripped them from his prostrate form whilst he'd been snoring away in an *ouzo* induced slumber.

"Cooee, Victor," Sherry called across the

garden, striding determinedly towards me, her progress somewhat impeded as her heels kept catching in the hem of the floating kaftan monstrosity she was wearing. Shuddering in horror, I wondered what possessed her to pair vibrant orange with sun reddened skin. I reflected that Marigold would never be caught dead venturing out in public in anything so shapeless, but then again Sherry is rather squarely built, not having my wife's trim figure.

"I'm glad I spotted you out here. I didn't fancy risking my neck on that rather lethal stone staircase of yours in these heels," Sherry brayed, throwing her head back and exposing her horsey dentures.

"Hello, Sherry," I replied, attempting to squirm away before the double kisses she was threatening actually landed on my cheeks.

"Hello, there, I'm Sherry. And you are? Another one of Victor's relative perhaps," Sherry said, aiming her pout at Guzim. He appeared as equally keen as I to squirm away from her indiscrimately dropped kisses, possibly worried she may nip his flesh with her prominent incisors. The poor chap could end up having nasty flashbacks about being attacked by the ferocious guard dog.

"Ti?" Guzim said. *"Victor, pes tis oti eimai pantremenos."*

I attempted to disguise the snort I involuntarily let loose when Guzim demanded that I tell Sherry he was a married man. Before I had chance to explain he was spoken for, Sherry continued to prattle on.

"I do feel such a dunce that I never twigged that Barry was your brother-in-law," Sherry brayed. "One really doesn't expect the help to move in the same circles, but I suppose the social norms of the Shires don't apply over here."

"Oh, I still socialised with Barry back in England, despite his lowly occupation," I said sarcastically.

"Well, I suppose if you are related there's not much you can do about it," Sherry said. Really, the woman was not only insufferable, but completely obtuse. "I heard you were something big in gastronomic circles."

"I worked for the council…"

"Ah, a councillor, local politics and all that," Sherry gabbled. "Henry liked to dabble."

For a moment my mind went blank as I wondered who Henry was. Eventually I recalled he was Sherry's deceased older husband, the one who had been loaded enough to enable

Sherry to breeze through life without ever doing an honest day's work.

"I didn't finish the introductions. This is Guzim, my gardener, well, part time. He's from Albania; he won't be able to understand a word you say," I said, realising that once again I sounded like Basil Fawlty introducing Manuel from Barcelona.

"*Kalimera,*" Sherry shouted. Guzim backed away as though only a mad woman would wish him good morning during the evening. I could tell from the shifty look in his narrowed eyes that Sherry made him uncomfortable. I had noticed a tendency in Guzim to exhibit fear in the presence of dominating women. Violet Burke never failed to strike the fear of God into him, reducing him to a blob of quivering jelly.

"Guzim also does a bit of labouring, not to mention he has a burgeoning business empire selling chicken manure," I added, not bothering to correct Sherry's Greek. It might prove quite amusing if she used the same greeting at the party: she would certainly make an impression.

"Is there much call for that?" Sherry asked, reminding me that I had been bigging up Guzim's carrier bags of chicken droppings.

"Well, he manages to shift all the shit my

chickens produce," I said a tad bluntly, immediately regretting that the woman had driven me to speak so crudely. "Sorry, droppings."

"*Skata,*" Guzim interjected, backing away. "*Skata.*"

"What's that?" Sherry asked.

"Oh, just another Greek greeting," I lied. Already embarrassed by my impromptu use of coarse language, I had no intention of informing Sherry that Guzim had just provided the Greek translation of shit.

Chapter 22

A Scurrilous Accusation

"Do speed it up, Marigold. Sherry is waiting in the garden," I called out to my wife as I hurriedly grabbed the bag of tripe spurned by Barry. Recalling how Panos had told me that *patsas* was popular in a soup eaten as a hangover cure, I decided I may as well attempt to palm it off on Apostolos: if he overindulged on the wine during his name day celebration, he may well have a craving for a big pot of hangover soup tomorrow.

There was method in my madness. Our route to Apostolos' house did not pass any public bins and Marigold would have my innards if the tripe was still stinking out the fridge on our return. Also, I seemed to recall that I had heard Apostolos agreeing wholeheartedly with Nikos during the latter's constant assertions that shop bought wine was inferior muck that couldn't hold a candle to *spitiko*. The gift of *patsas* would save me the cost of a bottle of red.

Marigold rushed down to greet Sherry, the pair of them exchanging double air-kisses. Sherry clearly didn't have the traditional Greek greeting down pat since she left a smear of orange lipstick on Marigold's ear. Dressed in a pretty blue floral A-line frock, my wife looked quite lovely. Unsure of the dress code, she had hedged her bets by opting for something that could easily transition from day to evening wear, smart but not too over-the-top.

Making our way to the street, Sherry caught her heel in the hem of the shapeless kaftan again. Fortunately, she made a clumsy grab to link arms with Marigold rather than me, leaving me to stride on ahead. Marigold demanded to know what on earth I was thinking, taking the bag of tripe along to the party. After opining that my explanation was, "perfectly ridiculous," she demanded that I walk downwind of them.

Arriving at Apostolos' house, we joined a huddle of our Greek neighbours and a clowder of cats in the picturesque walled courtyard. The setting was colourfully adorned with floral plants sprouting from old olive oil tins, recycled with a coat of blue paint. A collection of rusted bicycles formed an incongruous and unsightly heap in one corner, but I had to admire Apostolos' initiative in creating a charming trestle table out of what appeared to be an old wooden door. The table, or door, groaned under the weight of bottles of beer and plastic bottles of *krasi*. Unusually for a Greek celebration, there was not only no sign of food but no tantalising aroma to hint at the possibility we may be fed.

It was immediately apparent that as the sole representatives of the British contingent, we were somewhat overdressed. I spotted Panos in one corner, still clad in the same clothes and the ever present wellies he had worn to the market. He was chatting to Spiros, who appeared to have ventured out to the party in a sleeveless undershirt. I may as well be brutally honest; just because the undertaker is my good friend there is no point in beating about the bush to spare his feelings. Spiros had apparently decided to dress down in a vest, as in underwear. Despite his mafia shades, I had never seen him looking so uncharacteristically scruffy.

I made a beeline for Apostolos, desperate to unload the rank bag of stinking tripe as soon as possible. I must confess to being somewhat surprised when Apostolos grabbed the bag with genuine enthusiasm, burying his nose in deep and inhaling the vile smell with obvious relish. By now the smell was so putrid that I began to suspect the feet may have turned in the heat, but I decided to say nothing. Apostolos was obviously more au fait with the customary smell of sheep's feet than I. Clearly thrilled by the contents of the bag, he grabbed hold of my shoulders, planting a smacker of a kiss on my forehead, his wax stiffened moustache scraping across my skin like sandpaper. I reflected that it would serve him right if he ended up with marmite smeared in his tash.

"Victor, this is the, how to say in the English, the *kalos*?" Apostolos said.

"Good…"

"Yes, it is the good. I see the, how to say in the English, the *podia*?"

"The feet…"

"The feet, yes, they make the, how to say in the English, the *nostimo*?"

"Delicious…"

"Yes, the delicious. Between the you and the me, the wife not to allow the *podia* in the, how to say in the English, the *kouzina*?"

"The kitchen…"

"Yes, the kitchen. But I…" Apostolos paused dramatically, stabbing a finger at his chest to leave me in no doubt that the 'I' in question was most definitely him, "I will to cook the *patsas* and the *podia* outside on the, how to say in the English, the *fotia*?"

"The fire," I said, desperately hoping that his plan to cook the abominable contents of the bag wasn't imminent. I would certainly have shot myself in the foot if he pressed a bowl of foot laden *patsas* on me before the end of the evening.

Before Apostolos could interrupt me again, I managed to get more than a word of translation in.

"But I thought all good Greek wives liked to cook up huge pots of soup."

"Soup, what is this the soup in the Greek?"

"*Soupa…*"

"Yes, the soup, but the wife refuse to cook

the, how to say in the English, the *podia*?"

"The feet," I reminded him, deducing he had a memory like a sieve. "What is your wife's objection to cooking feet?"

"She think they are the not, how you to say in the English, the *ygienos*?"

"Hygienic. She certainly has a point. I wouldn't fancy eating something that an animal has been walking around on. Goodness knows what kind of filth it may have trod in."

"This is the best gift of the all. You must to come for the free, how to say in the English, the *kourema*?"

"I've no idea how that translates," I lied, having no intention of committing to one of Apostolos' lop-sided haircuts even if it was free. "Do excuse me. I need to speak to Spiros."

As I edged away, Apostolos shouted after me, "Yes, the *avrio* I to cook the big pan of the, how to say, the legs?"

Joining Spiros, I raised my eyebrows in wry amusement at the sight of his unruly chest hairs visibly sprouting from the top of his once white vest.

"I see the look you to give me, Victor," Spiros said. "All the other my dress is in the washing machine to be the clean when the Sampaguita arrive the tomorrow."

"Well, I hope you don't turn up at airport wearing that or Sampaguita will probably catch the next flight back to the Philippines," I chuckled.

"I will to ask the Marigold the advice on to wear the suit with the tie or without him for the reunite with the Sampaguita," Spiros confided. "I arrive early to the party so that the Apostolos can to give me the haircut."

"Ah, yes, I can see he's tidied you up," I said, observing Spiros' lopsided neckline. Recalling Spiros' usual vanity, I added, "I thought you only had your hair cut in town."

"There was no the time, I have been the busy with the funerals. I not want to drive the coffins to the airport."

Very wise, I thought to myself. With his mafia sunglasses, Spiros may well be mistaken for a dodgy dealer running drugs or AK47s inside his cargo if he turned up at the airport transporting a load of caskets.

"I really appreciate you collecting my mother whilst you are at the airport, Spiro. You truly are a wonderful friend."

"*Tipota*. For some the strange reason my fragrant Filipina flower has the taken the liking for the Violet Burke."

"There's no accounting for taste," I nodded sagely.

"After I collect the Sampaguita and the Violet Burke, I take them into the Athens to show them how our great Hellenic nation make the prepare for the Olympic Games," Spiros said.

"From what I've been reading, the centre of Athens is a bit of a nightmare to drive round at the moment. Maybe you'd be better off bypassing it whilst it resembles a giant construction site," I advised.

"This is the nonsense, Victor. We Greek make the great progress to welcome the world..."

Spiros was cut short as Sherry pushed between us. Whilst I plastered a fake smile on my face, girding my mental loins to be jollied, Sherry wished Spiros what she thought was a cheery Greek good evening.

"*Skata,*" Sherry said loudly, confident in her pronunciation of only the second Greek word she had mastered during her two month sojourn in the village.

"The other dress is in the washing machine," Spiros responded, presumably thinking Sherry had made a disparaging comment about the state of his vest. Taking the interruption in his stride, Spiros continued to talk about the Olympic Games that were scheduled to take place in Athens in just six weeks.

"I think the Sampaguita would to enjoy to see where the athlete from the Philippine will to the compete. The Sampaguita to say the whole of her the country is proud that their the countrymen will to compete in the national sport of the wongo. She to think they will to take the gold."

"The wongo?" I said, a tad puzzled. "That's a new one on me, Spiro, but as I may have mentioned, I'm not a great one for sport."

"I think you mean taekwondo," Sherry butted in.

"No, that is not the correct, but maybe the wongo he not the correct too," Spiros said, his bushy eyebrows almost obscuring his mafia sunglasses as he furrowed his brow in deep concentration. "Yes, I have it now, the sport is the haiku."

"A haiku is a Japanese poem, Spiros," I protested.

"You are the sure, Victor?"

"Most definitely," I confirmed.

"Then it must be that the Japanese admire

the Filipino sport of the wongo so the much that they make the poem about him," Spiros declared.

"It's taekwondo, not wongo, and it originated in Korea, not the Philippines," Sherry brayed.

Catching my eye, Spiros rolled his in an easily interpretable gesture that indicated Sherry was quite insufferable. After all, no one likes a know-it-all.

Clearly bored of our company and our ignorance of Korean sports, Sherry wandered off in Panos' direction, leaving Spiros and I to continue our chat. My attempts to persuade Spiros to steer clear of the centre of Athens fell on deaf ears. As a proud Hellene he was determined to show the Olympic venues off to the love of his life and my mother.

Marigold sauntered over to join us. After greeting Spiros with the customary kiss, she hissed in my ear, "Victor, I'm a tad worried that Sherry may have set her sights on Panos. I must make it clear to her that I have him earmarked for Violet Burke.

"I thought that you were convinced that Panos is sweet on Vi. Did I tell you that he put a sack of his best frying potatoes on one side for her? He certainly doesn't strike me as the playboy Casanova type," I assured her.

"I expect you're right, dear. Those dreadful wellies are hardly the footwear one would expect from a serial philanderer."

Marigold nudged me sharply in the ribs, nodding towards Sherry who was wandering around, still unattached, "Sherry hasn't latched onto Panos after all, thank goodness. That leaves the field free for your mother."

"I thought you were going to introduce Sherry to some eligible singles."

"They appear to be in rather short supply," Marigold said, glancing round in desperation as though she could suddenly magic up a quota of suitable bachelors to dangle in front of Sherry. Nikos and Dina had just arrived with their son Kostis in tow, and Kyria Kompogiannopoulou and Litsa were chatting with a group of pensioner fellows, none of whom struck me as sprightly enough to be able to entertain even the hope of a dalliance.

"You don't suppose one of those…" I suggested.

Rolling her eyes, Marigold interrupted, "I suppose if things gets desperate enough."

"It's early yet, there's still time for someone

a tad more eligible to turn up," I reassured her.

"Oh look, there's Papas Andreas," Marigold hissed as the local cleric walked in, arm and arm with his mother. "He's single now that Geraldine is walking out with that sexually infected chap."

"Andreas is single because he is a man of God who took a vow of chastity," I hissed back. "Anyway, does he even know that Geraldine has ditched him?"

"She's not plucked up the courage to tell him yet; she thought it too delicate a matter to blurt down the telephone."

"Well, don't encourage her to break the news in a letter or he'll be straight round to ours expecting me to translate the 'Dear John' for him," I winced. "Now, you know I'm not one to interfere, but I think in this instance that you rather need to bite the bullet and break the news to him. Otherwise, we'll be walking on eggshells every time we bump into him. It wouldn't do for him to find out during the baptism when he's conducting his official duty."

"I'm afraid that you're right, Victor. Whilst I hate the thought of having to do Geraldine's dirty work for her, we can't leave him hanging on obliviously…it's just not right. Now, do you want to break the news to him alone or would you prefer me to go over there with you?"

"Leave me out of it. She's your fickle friend. I'm having nothing to do with it."

"Hmm, I was afraid you'd say that," Marigold said in a resigned tone, recognising my immovable stance. "I suppose I might as well get it over with, no time like the present. And if he doesn't take it too badly, he may welcome Sherry consoling him if I can't dredge up someone else for her.

"What bit of celibate cleric do you not get?" I asked in exasperation.

I was wasting my time, talking to myself. Marigold had already stalked off, determination etched on her features. Sherry immediately edged in to take her place, having found no one more suitable to latch onto. Luckily, a fortuitous arrival saved me from being unwillingly jollied. Spotting Barry walk in, I made my excuses to Sherry, saying, "I'd better go and greet my brother-in-law. No, don't tag along; it wouldn't do for you to have to mix with the help."

I was pleased to see that Barry had managed to persuade Cynthia to venture out and even more delighted to spot baby Anastasia strapped to Barry's chest in a baby carrier. I considered that it was a good job that Marigold's back was turned or she would have dropped Papas Andreas like a hot potato, her mission unaccomplished, and rushed to coo over the baby.

"You look less stressed," I said to Barry as Cynthia wandered off to mingle.

"Yes, well, I've put my foot down. The next time Athena commands my presence, I'm sending Cynthia round." In response to my questioning eyebrow, Barry expounded, "Athena only went and answered the door with a thick splodge of white stuff over her lip. It seemed the polite thing to do to point out that she had what I thought was a milk moustache. You should have heard her carry on when she realised she'd opened the door without remembering to wash off her hair removal cream first. Some of her Greek expletives were new ones on me."

"So no more cosy confabs about *koufeta*..."

"What?"

"Sugared almonds," I translated. "I believe they are handed out at baptisms."

"Oh, right, I thought Athena just had a really sweet tooth. Things are starting to make more sense now."

"There you are my little cherub, oh, you're such a sweetie," Marigold gushed over the baby as she joined us, ignoring her brother and me.

"How did you get on with Papas Andreas? Did you dump him?" I asked.

"Yes, he took it remarkably well, very stoically. He didn't shed a single tear."

"Are you sure he understood you?"

"What's this?" Barry interrupted.

"Marigold's just dumped Andreas on Geraldine's behalf; she was never going to do it herself. It didn't seem right to string him along indefinitely," I explained.

"That man-mad woman has had more chaps than I've had hot dinners," Barry said.

"She just wants to find someone to settle down with, she's had a terrible time meeting a string of unsuitable men. Not everyone is as lucky in love as me and Victor, or you and Cynthia," Marigold admonished her brother. "Anyway, it's done now. I'll be glad to report back to Geraldine that Andreas didn't have a public breakdown. Once the dust has settled, she'll be able to fly over for a holiday with her new fellow."

I groaned aloud. Although I had encouraged Marigold to dump the cleric as it were, I had not expected that the upshot would mean giving house room to some tedious chap who would undoubtedly spend his holiday bending my ear about venereal diseases.

"Well, Andreas certainly appears to have moved on to pastures new with remarkable speed," Barry said. Glancing over, I noticed that the esteemed cleric was holding court to a captivated audience of one, Sherry hanging on his every word.

"Well, really. He could at least attempt to look heartbroken," Marigold peevishly complained.

"Perhaps he is simply offering her religious counsel," I suggested.

"Whatever Bible he uses must be a barrel of laughs," Barry quipped as the sound of Sherry's braying laughter reached us.

"It's most unseemly," Marigold remarked haughtily.

"You can't have it both ways. You were hoping you could let Andreas down gently on Geraldine's behalf and you dragged Sherry along hoping to fix her up with a new man. It looks to me as though you have successfully accomplished both your goals," I pointed out. Considering Marigold was on a mission to find her horsey friend a new partner, there was no logic to my wife flying into a sulk the minute a man showed an interest in Sherry.

"And I seem to remember you saying something earlier about Sherry possibly consoling the potentially broken hearted Andreas," I reminded Marigold.

"I only said that as an absolute last resort. I want to find her someone suitable. A dalliance with Andreas will lead exactly nowhere, as Geraldine discovered."

"Well, Sherry appears to be encouraging him," I pointed out.

"Victor, you must go and break it up," Marigold demanded.

Before I could object to my wife's demand, I was distracted by the unexpected arrival of Guzim, kitted out in my sweaty second-hand 'Body of a Greek God' tee-shirt paired with my muddy pyjama bottoms. I wondered if he had gate-crashed or was an invited guest.

"Oh, my goodness. I'm lost for words," Marigold said.

"Clearly not," I muttered under my breath.

"Hang on, Victor, isn't that the tee-shirt I gave you last Christmas?" Barry asked in an aggrieved tone.

"I doubt it was one of a kind," I hedged, hoping to put Barry off the scent. If he continued to catch me out giving away his unsuitable Christmas presents to my gardener, I would probably have nothing to unwrap by the time the festive season next rolled round. There again, considering Barry's horrendous taste, that might not be a bad thing.

Nursing a bottle of Amstel, Guzim cut a solitary figure, leaning on the trestle table and seemingly fixated on the sight of Papas Andreas and Sherry engaging in what appeared to be a scintillating conversation. I considered he was likely keeping a wary eye in case Sherry made a beeline for him and attempted to kiss him again. Taking a gulp of his beer, Guzim slammed the bottle down on the table and marched over to the couple, confronting the Papas with a scurrilous accusation that was loud enough to reach my ears.

I couldn't believe what I was hearing. My part-time gardener had just accused the respected cleric of stealing his trousers. Whilst not one to generally monitor what the Papas chooses to wear beneath his vestment, the trousers in question were on full display, the black ecclesiastical dress being hitched up around Andreas's hips as he sprawled in a reclined deckchair. I could empathise: the heat generated by wearing two leg coverings must be beyond a tad uncomfortable, particularly when coupled with all his facial hair. It was bad enough suffering socks in this heat to protect my ankles from pesky mosquitoes.

Edging closer, I heard Andreas lay into Guzim in a contemptuous manner not usually associated with a man of the cloth. Jumping out of the deckchair, he confronted Guzim, shouting that it was bad enough that he had accused his elderly frail mother of stealing a tortoise without now making malicious and unfounded claims about him stealing the Albanian's pants.

Although I thought that referring to Kyria Maria as frail was a tad blinkered, I had to agree that the accusation that the Papas had stolen his own trousers was bang out of order. Guiltily realising that it was my own actions that had led to this rumpus, I rushed to intervene, reluctantly confessing my own miserable part in the whole sorry trouser saga. Fortunately, since Kyria Maria had given the *ouzo* soaked trousers a good washing, Andreas eventually saw the funny side. Guzim grudgingly admitted that he never even liked the trousers in the first place and much preferred the new ones I had given him earlier.

Seemingly oblivious to the fact that he was actually prancing round in a pair of pyjama bottoms, Guzim pointed at them. Treating us to a toothless grin, he boasted, "Mark and Spender. *Kala nai.*"

Clearly relieved that she could contribute something to the incomprehensible foreign conversation, Sherry brayed, "Gosh, old Marks and Sparks have gone a bit daring with their summer collection..."

Sherry abruptly stopped speaking mid-sentence: her mouth gaping, she stared across the room hungrily before grabbing my sleeve and hissing, "I say, Victor, who's that man over there? He's got a certain something about him that reminds me of my late Henry."

"I thought that you had the hots for the Papas," I said, craning my neck to see who had caught her attention.

"Don't be silly, I was just being polite to cover up my mortification for greeting him with a very rude word. Can you believe I said 'shit' to a vicar? Now, who is that man, Victor, the one chatting to the old widow?"

Ignoring her ignorance in confusing a Papas and a vicar, I finally spied who Sherry had her eye on and suppressed a snort. I'd never have guessed that the old garlic eating pensioner, Mathias, would remind Sherry of her late husband.

"Let me introduce you," I offered, thinking Marigold would be thoroughly delighted by this bizarre turn of events.

Chapter 23

Victor Did Warn Him

Checking the clock for the umpteenth time, I began to worry. It was now late afternoon and Spiros had been due to collect Sampaguita and Violet Burke at the airport first thing this morning, but there was still no sign of them. Having confirmed that both flights touched down on time, my imagination began to paint a doomsday scenario of the hearse being hideously mangled in a traffic accident. Marigold opined it was more likely that

Violet Burke had driven Spiros to distraction with endless talk of her swollen feet, leading to a murderous outcome where my mother took up permanent residence in one of his coffins. Whilst admittedly Marigold's scenario had legs, as anyone who has ever spent more than a couple of hours listening to my mother's many complaints could testify, her theory had a flaw. The hearse had been mercifully freed of any back seat caskets in order to make room for the luggage.

Although I had tried Spiros' mobile a couple of times without success, I was reluctant to continually bombard his number with calls. I would never forgive myself if by ringing his phone, I distracted Spiros from the road and he ended up causing a multiple-vehicle collision.

My constant pacing was beginning to wear on Marigold's nerves.

"For goodness sake, Victor, stop being such a worrywart. I expect Spiros simply stopped off somewhere to treat them to a leisurely lunch."

Marigold's words did nothing to ease my mind: I imagined Violet Burke driving Spiros to the *ouzo,* leading to the undertaker's arrest for being drunk in charge of a hearse.

Finally, after hours of anxious waiting,

Spiros phoned to say that he was almost at the village. Sighing with relief, Marigold immediately dashed off to Doreen's, saying that she didn't want to intrude on my possibly emotional reunion with Violet Burke. Even after thirty-seven years of marriage, Marigold never fails to surprise me with such thoughtful gestures. On the other hand, I mused, my wife could possibly be using Doreen as a convenient excuse to delay her own reluctant reunion with my mother, at least until all mention of swollen feet was safely out of the way.

Ambling down to the street to wait for the hearse, I walked into a veritable wall of heat, the humidity stiflingly muggy in its closeness, the silence of siesta time only broken by the persistent musical buzz of a million cicadas. A stray cat, sprawled out on the street side doorway of the *apothiki,* opened one lazy eye to observe me disinterestedly, too hot to move.

The *vasilikos* on Kyria Maria's doorstep visibly drooped in the humidity. Tempted though I was to turn her hosepipe on to revive it, I knew a sudden watering would likely scorch the basil and cause it to wither. It wouldn't do to be accused of killing off such a holy plant, particularly in light of the scurrilous accusations regarding the neighbouring household that Guzim had slanderously tossed around the previous evening.

Still, I reflected, the evening had ended on a high note. When it became apparent that Apostolos' wife's reluctance to cook feet appeared to extend to producing food of any kind, a most unnatural state of Greek affairs, Marigold and I adjourned to the taverna with Barry, whilst Cynthia took the baby home. Sherry, seemingly rather taken with Mathias, had preferred to linger at the party rather than join us, even though she was incapable of communicating with the local garlic eater.

Taking pity on Guzim, I invited him to join us, admittedly inspired by Sherry's shameful reluctance to hobnob with the help. Finding her attitude deplorable when it was directed towards my brother-in-law, I belatedly realised that I was a tad hypocritical to then harbour the same condescending attitude towards Guzim.

My gardener's grovelling prostration of gratitude to be included in our small gathering made me feel guilty that I had never previously included him socially. I felt a tad better when I recalled he had attended Barry's wedding, though I don't recall inviting him: most likely he gate-crashed. The impromptu taverna invitation I extended attracted a withering look from Marigold. My wife has had a low tolerance threshold for the Albanian shed dweller ever since she caught him gifting me my own fruit in the hope of procuring himself a bottle of breakfast Amstel.

The sound of a horn blasting in flagrant disregard of the silence expected during siesta hours brought me out of my reverie. As the hearse approached, I did a double take. Even though Sampaguita has luscious dark locks rather than blonde hair, something about the stilted way she and Spiros were perched in the car, erect and glassy eyed as though caught in the headlights, reminded me of Lady Penelope and Aloysious Parker in the 60s television series Thunderbirds. Actually, it was odd that I had never noticed the striking resemblance between Spiros' eyebrows and those of the puppet chauffeur before.

As the hearse pulled up beside me, I saw Violet Burke's bulbous form took centre place between the recently reunited lovebirds. The way she was so prominently squashed between them barely left any room for Spiros to turn the steering wheel and flattened Sampaguita against the side window pane. The pair appeared rather shell shocked, perhaps understandable if my mother had kept up a running commentary outlining all her aches and pains on the long drive from Athens.

Sampaguita was the first to alight, smiling in genuine pleasure as she took in the familiar village sights.

"Hello, Mr Bucket…"

"Victor, please, no need for formality. It is good to see you again, Sampaguita."

"It is good to be back," she said. "I must help Mrs Burke; she seems to be stuck in the seat."

"Not enough room to swing a cat," my mother complained as her swollen feet hit the pavement, helped out of the hearse by Spiros pushing her bulbous form from one side whilst Sampaguita pulled from the other.

"Hello Victor, I hope you've got the kettle on, I'm fair parched. I thought we were never going to get here. Spiros insisted on taking the long way round through that bloody construction site."

"Hello, Mother. What construction site?" I asked, presuming that Vi was confusing road works with building work.

"I think she means Athens," Sampaguita said.

"The road in the Athens was the chaos," Spiro groaned.

"I did warn you not to go into the centre," I reminded him.

"I want to show off the great Hellenic capital and the many new building for to host the Olympic Games. How I to know the road the full of the hole and the traffic not to move? It is not as if the game he kick off today, it is still more the month and the half to the opening," Spiros shouted, using his hands expressively to drive home his points.

"Well, you might have wanted to drive us round the city, but you didn't do much driving, did you? Stuck in a dusty hot traffic jam for hours we were, Victor, with no facilities in sight if you get my drift," Vi complained.

"I drive you to the house of the cousin second to use the toilet," Spiros cried in exasperation. "Never I know the woman to need the toilet so many the time, it must be the British tea he drink."

I have to confess it rather amused me to hear Spiros do such an about face. Only yesterday he had been certain that I was exaggerating when I warned him to avoid the centre of Athens. Now, instead of boasting about his great capital city, he was full of complaints.

"Get my bags, Victor. I can't stand out here gassing all day, I need a cuppa," my mother ordered, before turning to kiss Sampaguita on the cheek. "Don't be a stranger now, you hear. I'll pop over tomorrow with the mushy peas; they're at the bottom of the case."

Turning to me, Vi said, "Can you believe the poor child has never tasted a mushy pea?"

"I will be happy to see you, Mrs Burke. I will make you the Fukien tea," Sampaguita said with a smile.

"I've told you to call me Violet, but there's no need for that sort of language. I can always bring some Tetley's round," my mother retorted.

"The Fukien tea is tea from the Philippines," Sampaguita clarified.

"Well, I suppose it won't hurt to try it but I hope it's nothing like that horrible stuff Maria serves. Full of floating twigs, it is."

Wearily hauling her bulbous form up the outside stairs, Vi called out over her shoulder, "Victor, do get a move on with my bags, I'm gagging for a Warrington egg."

Turning to Spiros and Sampaguita, I thanked them profusely for putting up with my mother.

"I like Mrs Burke, but perhaps in smaller doses," Sampaguita said, a twinkle in her eye.

Despite the lovebirds having been stuck with my mother ever since they were reunited, Spiros seemed in no hurry to rush away, determined to vent about the state of things in Athens.

"The hole, Victor, you would not to believe him. The hole in the road so big enough to hold the Olympic opening ceremony. They to make the potholes in Meli look like *tipota*. And so much the money they spend. What the for? For the security they to say, but I not to trust them. You know they throw the money at the frogmen with the AK47, I think they to get the gun from the *Alvaniki* mafia. And everywhere they make the camera to spy on the proud Hellenic citizen."

"I read that the cameras were a security precaution for the Olympics, Spiro," I said, recalling my friend liked nothing more than a half-baked conspiracy theory.

"You think the camera to disappear when the Greece win the Olympic, no they keep him to spy on us. You say the camera to make the Athens safe, Victor. I say, but at what the cost to our liberty? We Greek never to forget, *'Eleftheria i Thanatos.*"

"I think you are overreacting a tad, Spiro," I said, thinking that a few security cameras popping up in Athens hardly represented a challenge to the avowed Greek belief in 'Freedom or Death.'

"Ah, but I show them, you see. I get out from the hearse and hold my business card under the camera. Perhaps many the people dead in the Olympic from the frogmen shooting the AK47, but now the camera he see my business card. I can to do the funeral in the Athens, big money."

"Very enterprising of you," I said, suppressing a snort as I wondered what the security operatives manning the camera feeds would make of a suited undertaker in mafia sunglasses ranting in the street and waving his business card.

"And you know, Victor, they to spend all the money on the Athens but nothing on the Meli. All the security there and not the one policemen here."

"Well, to be fair, there isn't any crime in Meli," I pointed out.

"You are the wrong. Only yesterday the evening I hear the Andreas say the someone to steal his trousers. Imagine the bold thief to steal from the man of the God. It is how you say in English, the start of the greasy slope."

"The slippery slope," I corrected, beginning to see how rumours managed to get so ridiculously out of hand in the village.

"Victor, my bags," my mother hollered down, poking her head through the window.

"Coming," I dutifully responded. Grabbing my mother's cases, I turned to proffer some advice to Spiros. "Forget all about Athens and such inconsequential things. Now that you are finally reunited with Sampaguita, it is time to concentrate on romance."

"Yes, I have the propose to do," Spiros said, the frustration on his face replaced with a determined but soppy look.

Chapter 24

Fray Bentos and Swollen Feet

"Chuck a Fray Bentos in the oven, Victor. My stomach fair thinks my throat's been cut," Violet Burke demanded, depositing her sizeable bulk on a kitchen chair with a weary sigh. "I'd never have had that Spiros down as such a pernickety fusspot; he flatly refused to let me snack on my sausage roll in the car. You'd think he'd have made an exception with it being a Greek one."

"He maintains the highest of standards in

the hearse. Even though he is generally most obliging, he wouldn't even let Marigold transport her precious felines to the vet in his pristine vehicle," I said in defence of the local undertaker.

"You can hardly compare a sausage roll to a cat," my mother huffed.

"They both shed things that aren't ideal around dead bodies," I said. My mother frowned in puzzlement. "Pastry crumbs and cat hairs," I elaborated.

"But he didn't have a corpse in the back," my mother stated. "Here, pass me that little case, Victor. I smuggled some Warrington eggs over. I'll have a couple while I wait for the steak and kidney to heat up. Help yourself, lad, you're looking a bit on the thin side."

I wasn't surprised that mother had travelled armed with her favourite northern delicacy of pickled eggs coated in black pudding, dipped in beer batter and deep fried. Recalling they were actually quite tasty, I was tempted to tuck in, until I recalled Marigold's warning that they would play havoc with my cholesterol levels. As if reading my mind, Violet Burke asked, "Where's that wife of yours?"

* * *

"Marigold has called round to visit her friend Doreen; she thought that we'd appreciate some mother and son alone time," I said, taking advantage of Marigold's absence to reach for a prohibited Warrington egg. "How was the journey over?"

"It was a slog and no mistake. I sometimes wonder why I bother. It's too much hassle just for a week or two. My poor feet will only just have time to deflate before they get all swelled up again on the journey home. Look at the state of them."

"Nasty," I agreed, eyeing the bulging flesh encased in wrinkled nylon spilling over the sides of her sensible flat lace-ups.

"Swollen something shocking they are. Pass me the washing up bowl. I need to give them a good soaking before they explode."

"You may want to hold off on that, Vi. I've had an outdoor spa installed since your last visit. You'll be able to soak your feet to your heart's content. Just don't go mentioning it to Maria next door."

"So what if I do? She can't understand a word that I say anyway, not that she's not good company," she said, sinking her teeth into a Warrington egg with obvious relish. "In fact as soon as I've got some food in my stomach, I will pay her a visit. I've got something to show her. Pass me my handbag, Victor."

Rummaging round in her enormous handbag, Vi began to remove some of the travel detritus she had carted over to Greece. A garish pink plastic object with a large button caught my eye. Intrigued, I asked, "What's that?"

"It's my rape alarm. I thought it would come in handy over here on account of the goats. It should get rid of them sharpish if they start chewing on the washing."

Relieved to hear that she hadn't carted it to Greece on account of any unwanted amorous advances by the local men, I reflected if Guzim had carried a similar device on his person it might have seen Apollo off before it had chance to sink its fangs into his bottom. A clear plastic rain hat, an overdue library book and an unopened packet of compression socks piled up next to the rape alarm.

"You're supposed to wear these on the flight, not stash them in your handbag," I told her. "It's no wonder your feet swelled up."

"I knew I'd put them somewhere handy, oh

well, I can try them out on the flight back," Vi said pragmatically. "Ooh no, I've got lard on my library book. That will need a good disinfecting before I take it to bed."

"How have you managed to get lard on it?" I asked, perplexed.

"This has leaked," my mother replied, holding up a dented packet of lard, the thick greasy contents oozing out round the edges. My mind boggled, imagining how she had managed to smuggle the lard through airport customs. Since she is clearly an expert at couriering illicit goods through foreign borders, I should have given her a last minute call and asked her to smuggle some honeysuckle tripe over for Barry.

"Got it," Vi exclaimed triumphantly, produced an envelope smeared with both lard and chip fat.

My curiosity admittedly piqued, I asked, "What have you got in there?"

"Photos of fish," she replied. "I thought they would be a bit of an ice-breaker for me and Maria. I can tell her the English words for the fish and she can tell me what they are in Greek. We might as well start somewhere. We share a liking for eating fish, even if Maria does have the disgusting habit of cooking them with their heads still on."

"An excellent idea," I agreed.

"Dot in the chippy took these photos with her camera, do you fancy a gander?"

Taking the envelope from my mother, I bit down on my lip to suppress my involuntary smirk of amusement. Expecting to see photographs of actual fish swimming in the ocean, I was rather taken aback to see that Dot had photographed the battered and breaded deep fried offerings that they served up in the chippy.

Leaning over my shoulder, Vi provided a running commentary, "See, that's the cod and that's the haddock. That one's the plaice. Dot couldn't get a good likeness of the scampi. Oh, I don't know how that one of a battered sausage got in, I'm sure Maria knows what a sausage is."

"I'm sure she'll appreciate it, after all she has no idea that a *loukaniko* is a sausage in English," I said.

"Fancy calling a sausage something that sounds like a portaloo," my mother chuckled. Reminding me that she was still in desperate need of my washing up bowl, she threatened to ease her poor swollen feet with lard if I didn't hand it over. The thought was too disgusting to contemplate so I reluctantly filled the bowl with hot water, making a mental note to invest in yet another spare.

"I'll take the rest of the Warrington eggs round to Maria when I go over. I have to remember not to overindulge, doctor's orders."

"I didn't know you were under the doctor, you never mentioned it on the phone," I said, my voice thick with worry. Despite her constant complaints about her swollen feet and numerous aches, Violet Burke always struck me as being in robust health.

"The cheeky gobdaw gave me a right lecture on how I need to lose weight to ease the strain on my swollen feet. I had better rations during the war than he'd have me on now," she practically spat.

"It might be worth listening to him, you do tend to suffer with your feet," I said tactfully, thinking that she did look a tad more bulbous than usual.

"Happen as maybe, but he can swing if he thinks I'd going on any diet that bans chips," Vi said emphatically.

"Remember I told you that my recently discovered half-brother Douglas is over in Greece at the moment…"

"I've not lost my marbles yet," Vi interrupted.

"Well, his wife Elaine runs her own very successful diet club, perhaps she could give you some pointers," I suggested. "We'll be meeting up with them for dinner later."

"I'm perfectly capable of cutting back without some diet guru interfering," she insisted. "I'll start now by just having half of the Fray Bentos; you look like you need feeding up."

Before I could give in to the temptation of half a cholesterol raising tinned pie, Marigold returned. My wife plastered a broad smile on her face at the sight of Violet Burke, a smile that quickly faded when she noticed my mother had planted her swollen feet in the washing up bowl. Whilst Marigold may consider some of my hygiene quirks a tad wearing, nothing quite turns her stomach more than the washing up bowl being turned into an impromptu foot spa.

"How was your journey, Vi?" Marigold asked.

"Hot and squashed. That Spiros doesn't have much to say for himself..."

"He probably couldn't get a word in edgeways," I muttered.

"And have you seen the state of my feet? Look how they've all swelled up."

"You should try wearing compression socks

on the flight," Marigold advised. "Anyway, I've got something nice that will take your mind off your feet. I bought you a lovely hat to wear for the baptism."

"Oh, there's nothing I like more than a nice new hat," Violet Burke gushed.

Marigold disappeared to unearth the hat, returning in a jiffy with the exotic millinery that resembled a fruit bowl. As she waved it in front of Vi with a flourish, my mother's face fell. Adopting a querulous tone, she complained, "I can't say I've a fancy for straw hats, being ten a penny they're a bit common. I have to say I'd have preferred something with a bit more style, something that made a bit more of a statement."

"You can't fail to make a statement in that glorified fruit bowl," I quipped.

"I suppose it will have to do, I doubt there's a massive selection of hats to be had in the middle of nowhere," Violet Burke grumbled in a resigned tone. "But it will need some adjustments."

"I'm sure we can remove some of the plastic fruit if you think it's a bit much," Marigold offered.

"Oh no, the fruit gives it a proper voguish look, it's all that common straw that I can't abide.

Happen you could pluck a few feathers from those chickens of yours, Victor. We could stick them over the straw with a bit of superglue."

"Feathers and fruit would be quite the combination," I chuckled. Noticing the withering look that Marigold was firing in my direction, I hastily added, "But what do I know? I'm certainly no authority on women's fashion."

Catching up over a cuppa whilst Vi waited for the Fray Bentos to puff up, we were surprised to receive an unexpected visitor. I hadn't expected Panos to be so quick off the mark in calling on my mother. Without bothering to remove his wellies, the farmer marched into the kitchen, carrying a large pan.

"*Yassou* Violeta," he said, his face reddening just a tad.

"Tell him the name's Violet straight, tell him not to go poncifying it," my mother barked. "I'm a bit long in the tooth to start answering to something new and Violeta doesn't half sound pretentious."

"*I mitera mou protima Violet, ochi Violeta,*" I said, at a loss how I could even begin to offer a translation of poncifying: I wasn't convinced such a word even existed.

"*Echo patsas yia sena,*" Panos said.

"What's he got in that pan, Victor?" my mother asked.

"Tripe soup. We were discussing it yesterday and now it seems he has brought me a pan of the stuff to try."

"Hmm, a man who can cook," my mother said in surprise, as though it was something unusual. I don't think she appreciates just how much I do in the kitchen.

"Fetch it over here," she demanded. Lifting the lid, she took a hearty sniff. "Don't worry lad, we can sling it out when my gentleman caller has left. If I let you eat that, likely you'll have to have your stomach pumped."

"*Ti leei*?" Panos asked what she was saying.

"She says the soup looks delicious. We'll try it later, we just had eggs," I said in Greek.

"What are you telling him, Victor?" my mother asked, prompting me to repeat my words in English for her benefit.

"I never said it looked delicious, Victor. You need to wash your ears out. I said if you eat that vile smelling concoction you'll have to have your stomach pumped."

Cringing inwardly, I decided to put a stop to this. I had no intention of being used as a convenient translator.

"Pano, kathise. Marigold kai ego pigainoume yia mia volta." Inviting Panos to take a seat, I told him that Marigold and I were going out for a walk. "We'll leave you to it, Mother, just off for a walk."

"But what about the Fray Bentos?"

"Share it with Panos."

As Marigold and I beat a hasty retreat, Marigold commended me on my sensitivity in leaving the pair alone.

"I can see the matchmaking bug is rubbing off on you, dear."

Chapter 25

The Ex-Pat Book Club

Returning to the house, Marigold insisted we stomp up the stairs to announce our presence, wary we may blunder in and interrupt a romantic interlude. Clearly my wife was projecting her own deluded fantasy onto the pensioner pair.

Panos was installed at the kitchen table tucking into Fray Bentos with apparent gusto, his wellies off, his socks in need of a good darning. Between mouthfuls of pie, Violet Burke was talking at him, blustering on even though Panos could not comprehend a word she was saying.

"Sou aresei i konservopolimeni pita?" I said, asking Panos if he liked the tinned pie.

"Einai nostimo." I was surprised to hear him declare the Fray Bentos pie delicious. Like many of the locals, Panos was very vocal about considering foreign food inferior to the exclusively Greek food he had been raised on in his grandmother's kitchen. Violet Burke abruptly announced she was popping over to visit Maria next door. Stuffing his feet back into his wellies, Panos gallantly walked her out, prompting Marigold to spy on them from the balcony just in case their farewell took a romantic turn.

"I've no idea how they manage to communicate," Marigold huffed, clearly disappointed that Panos hadn't dropped down on one knee on the pavement and whipped out a ring.

Having arranged to meet Douglas and his family down on the coast for pre-dinner drinks, I made a point of arriving early. Since none of us had the slightest interest in football, I wanted to secure a table in one of the seafront café bars that wasn't blasting the UEFA semi-final between

Greece and the Czech Republic on a widescreen television. It struck me that it would be impossible to engage in meaningful conversation if we had to compete with the boisterous din of football fans. Although I would have enjoyed entertaining Douglas in our local taverna, I knew that Nikos had been persuaded to screen the game on his old television set.

"We could eat here, Victor. There's a garden in the back the children could play in, rather than expecting them to sit still in a taverna," Marigold suggested as our drinks arrived.

"It suits me," Violet Burke agreed. "The chairs are almost comfy and it would save me traipsing around on my swollen feet. Pass me a menu, Victor, I'll have a look and see if they do chips."

I was amazed that my mother could even consider menu options so soon after polishing off Warrington eggs and a Fray Bentos.

"Good, they do chips," my mother announced after perusing the menu which fortunately offered an English translation.

"Maria is certainly skilled with the knitting needles," Marigold said, admiring the new cardigan Violet Burke was wearing. Crafted in blue and white wool, it made mother look like a walking emblem for the Greek nation, though goodness knows how she could tolerate such a bulky covering in the heat.

"To think Maria knitted this cardie for me, proper lovely it is. You could have blown me away when she gave it to me. I was that embarrassed though, I hadn't thought to bring her a present from England. Luckily, I remembered I still had those compression socks in my handbag, so I made out I'd got them especially for her. It was either that or my library book."

Relaxing in the café bar, I began to feel the stress of the day fading away. Tuning out the sound of Marigold and Vi's chatter, I drank in the sea view and engaged in a spot of people watching. There were lots of Greek men walking along the seafront sporting the green team shirts of *Panathinaikos,* a club that attracted popular support from the locals. Even though I have no interest in football, I have astutely cottoned on that "*Panathinaikos*" is the correct answer to trot out when I am regularly asked what team I support, "*Ti omada*?" My avowed support for the team always goes down well and helps in my endeavour to be accepted as one of the locals.

My musings were interrupted by Vi demanding that I fetch her some water because she was overheating.

"Perhaps you'd be a tad cooler without the cardie," I suggested, going to the bar for water like a dutiful son. Placing the order, I glanced around. You could have knocked me down with a feather when I noticed that one of the patrons had a copy of 'Delicious Desire' openly displayed on the table in front of her. Immediately recognising the book as Milton's published porn, I thought how shameless to make no attempt to hide such smutty reading matter in a brown paper wrapping. Rather intrigued, I edged a tad closer, realising to my surprise that the woman's female companions also had copies of the book: most likely one of them was the woman that Milton had pegged as his stalker.

Recognising one of the group as the emaciated wife of *Terastios* Hugh, I used our market *vlita* connection as an excuse to intrude, making an amusing quip that I hoped I wasn't interrupting a meeting of the local ex-pat book club.

"That's exactly what we are," Hugh's wife responded with delight, immediately introducing herself as Sandra, and her companions as Bessie, Iris and Jane. Apart from Bessie, they all welcomed me warmly. Radiating smug superiority, Bessie's unattractive face was framed with steel grey hair shaped like a helmet and in desperate need of a good styling from Athena. She looked me up and down with a sour expression as though she had just been force fed the contents of a pickle jar. Before she even opened her mouth, I took an instant, visceral dislike to her.

"That looks a tad risqué for a book club pick," I said to the group, pretending I had never seen it before.

"It was Sandra's choice, apparently she missed the point about us selecting works of literature," Bessie piped up. "I told them we should limit ourselves to novels on the Booker shortlist."

"Well, I'm glad I chose it. It's a good read, perfect for the beach. And there's no harm in picking up a few ideas to spice up life in the bedroom," Sandra said.

"Well, I think at our age, we should be past all that kind of nonsense," Bessie opined in a voice infused with inflated self-importance. Considering the group appeared to be my age, I was glad that Marigold didn't share her opinion.

"Speak for yourself, some of us are still in

our prime," Jane muttered under her breath, giving me a saucy wink, whilst worriedly checking that Bessie hadn't heard. It struck me that the group appeared a tad intimidated by Bessie.

"The book hardly reflects well on our feminist credentials and I have never heard of the publisher. Most likely third-rate," Bessie said in a dismissive tone intended to put the others in their place and let them know what she considered they should think important.

"I have to say, I'm quite enjoying 'Delicious Desire' It's a bit titillating though; I have to hide it from my husband," Iris said.

"I've been leaving my copy lying around in the hope that it will give Hugh some ideas," Sandra admitted.

"My first choice would have been a book about living in Greece. I do like to read tales of other Brits moving abroad," Iris said.

"My wife is an addict of such books…"

"Oh, spare me the boring ramblings of British ex-pats. Books like that can hardly be considered proper literature," Bessie interrupted, her tone oozing disdain. "Anyone who has moved here could knock one out, but it doesn't make them real writers that have studied the craft. Personally, I am honing my writing skills by studying a book that tells one how to write the great novel."

"But a true storyteller is born, not made," I bristled, not in the least impressed by Bessie's literary pretentions.

"I disagree; one must study and abide by the rules. It takes years to perfect one's prose. The most important thing isn't the story; it is abiding by the 'show, not tell', rule. As for this piece of third rate garbage," Bessie held up a copy of Milton's book, "The publisher should have gone through it with a fine tooth comb to remove every last adverb. Everyone knows adverbs have no place in proper literature."

Bessie stood up and pushed by me, heading off in the direction of the toilets. For someone with such an inflated opinion of herself, her short stumpy stature took me by surprise, her disproportionally large bust threatening to tip her over face first. Her companions visibly relaxed as soon as she vacated her chair.

"Perhaps your wife would be interested in joining our book club," Iris suggested, most likely keen to get another fan of moving abroad books on side to outvote Bessie's selection of what they ought to be reading.

"I'm afraid my wife has a very low tolerance

for being bossed about," I said, indicating the now vacated chair with a sleight of hand. "But I will certainly mention it to Sherry. She recently moved to our village and is jolly keen to join expat clubs." I rather imagined that Sherry would be more than capable of cutting the conceited Bessie down to size and I couldn't imagine for one moment that she'd be voting for anything highbrow enough to make the Booker shortlist.

Spotting Bessie heading back, I beat a hasty retreat, quite tempted to send Violet Burke over to do her worst. Milton would be over the moon when I relayed that his porn was the monthly choice for the local book club. I suppose I ought to have defended his tome a tad more, but in fairness I hadn't been able to bring myself to read it, the page that the cat had destroyed appearing total guff. At least he needn't worry there was any possibility of smug Bessie being his stalker.

Chapter 26

Egg and Chips

"Uncle Bucket, Uncle Bucket." The excited cries of the twins announced the arrival of my new family. Douglas and Violet Burke had of course met at Vic's funeral, but Elaine and the twins had not yet had the pleasure of meeting my mother. The girls appeared quite taken with Violet Burke, no doubt drawn to her pragmatic and no-nonsense way of addressing them. They practically begged for a closer look at her swollen feet, positively transfixed by the way the flesh bulged so squishily over the sides of her shoes. It reminded me of the way they had been so fascinated by my tales of kitchen gore.

"If we poke it, will it wobble like jelly?" Millie asked, unabashedly testing her theory.

"Uncle Bucket got cross when we gave his cats a bath in jelly," Tilly blurted.

"It made the cats spit bubbles," Millie giggled.

Desperate to change the subject before Marigold could make the connection between bathing the cats in jelly and her now empty bottle of posh shower gel, I urged everyone to decide what they would like to eat. An almost unanimous decision was reached to order Greek salad and chips all round, with a side order of *tzatziki* and *tirokafteri,* Violet Burke the only stubborn holdout. Refusing to eat salad swimming in oil, she announced that she would have an extra plate of chips instead.

"But you told me your doctor warned you to cut back and watch your diet," I reminded her, a tad concerned that I should be worried about her health.

"Fine, I'll just have one portion. It's a good job I've still got that sausage roll in my handbag,

I hope it hasn't turned."

"I wouldn't risk a sausage roll that hasn't been refrigerated, Mother. How long has it been in your bag?"

"All day. Happen you're right," she replied in a decidedly miffed tone. "Order me a couple of nice fried eggs to go with my chips."

"They don't appear to offer fried eggs on the menu," I said.

"I'm sure you can persuade them. A fried egg is a fried egg, whether it's Greek or British," Vi pointed out, ever pragmatic.

Although I tend to think of Vi as bulbous, a visual image I conjured up long before meeting her, a more apt description would be solidly stout. On this occasion, in the flesh, my mother's stout shape appeared fleshier and less solid than usual. Picking up on my concern about Vi's health, Marigold flat out asked Vi if she'd put on some weight since her last visit. My wife is never one to beat about the bush.

"Well, what if I have? I need a bit of comfort eating. I'm about to lose my job in the chippy, not to mention my home."

"There's a lot of comfort to be found in the bottom of a bag of chips," Elaine said sympathetically. "It takes a lot of will power to change one's eating habits. I used to have a terrible weakness for chips with mayonnaise."

"I don't know how you could stomach the stuff," Violet Burke said, her face crumpled in disgust.

"Mayonnaise?" Elaine queried.

"You should thank your blessings that you never had to eat the mayonnaise muck we concocted out of wartime rations. Back then it was made out of flour, marg and sugar. And a bit of dried egg, if you could get your hands on any."

I cringed at the thought. The last time Marigold had been in the mood for prawn cocktail, I had whipped up the Marie Rose sauce from fresh egg yolks, extra virgin olive oil and a dash of Tabasco.

"Has the council come up with any alternative accommodation yet?" Marigold asked my mother.

"The only place they've come up with isn't suitable. I shall have to turn it down," she replied, a defiant edge to her tone.

"I suppose it's some dreadful high-rise?" I sighed, imagining a dreary flat and a broken lift reeking of urine.

"No, they found me a ground floor flat on account of my feet."

"Surely that's good," Marigold pointed out.

"There's nothing good about being expected to live next door to that miserable old harridan, Edna Billings," Vi retorted.

"Plaice on a Friday," I recollected.

"That's the one," Vi said glumly. I could sympathise. I couldn't imagine anything worse than being forced to live next door to Harold. I rather gathered that Mrs Billings was mother's equivalent of my Harold nemesis.

Our conversation was interrupted by Sandra stopping to say goodbye as she left, casually draping a hand on my shoulder. Feeling Marigold's hackles rise, I hastily whispered to my wife that the ex-pat book club had selected Milton's porn as their book of the month. Whilst Marigold's mouth gaped in surprise, I introduced Elaine to Sandra, announcing that Sandra's husband Hugh might well be a possible convert to Elaine's diet club. Amazingly, even on holiday, Elaine carried an impossible amount of diet bumph in her handbag, pressing her leaflets onto the eager ex-pat.

"Hugh could do with losing the odd stone or five if he's going to be inspired by 'Delicious Desire,'" Sandra giggled as she left.

"I have to confess that I very nearly let the

cat out of the bag about Milton," Marigold whispered to me.

"It wouldn't have been very discreet to let slip that the local pornographer is a neighbour of ours. Discretion is very important if I'm ever going to get away with digging out the old V.D. Bucket name," I reminded her.

"You're right, of course, dear," Marigold agreed. "Perhaps I should read Milton's book since it's becoming so popular."

"Not Milton's book, Scarlett Bottom's," I said with a wink.

"That makes it sound ten times worse," Marigold laughed. "I wonder where Milton came up with such a ludicrous pseudonym."

"Heaven knows," I fibbed, having no intention of confessing that I may have had more than a little to do with it.

"I really think you're onto something with your idea to incorporate more Greek inspired dishes into the diet plan," Elaine said to Douglas, tucking into her Greek salad with relish.

"I rather think that Victor's lettuce salad may be less calorific than this delicious mix of tomatoes, olives, peppers and feta," Douglas said. "What did you call it again, Victor?"

"*Maroulosalata.* It's just lettuce, spring onions and dill, with a dressing of olive oil and lemon."

"Maybe if I add a few olives it will liven it up," Elaine said hopefully.

From the corner of my eye, I spied smug Bessie and Iris approaching our table. Fortunately, they weren't heading in my direction specifically since our table was situated by their exit route. Nevertheless, I bristled on Violet Burke's behalf when I overhead smug Bessie say to her companion, "Fancy coming all the way to Greece to eat egg and chips. So unadventurous."

Quick as a flash, Violet Burke fired back, "Fancy being all smug and superior when you've got a face like a plate of slapped tripe."

I imagine my mother must have been inspired by Panos' delivery of revolting soup. Although it was juvenile, I inwardly applauded her quick-witted retort.

A group of impossibly attractive Greek youngsters ambled along the seafront, all wearing the green shirts or scarves of the popular football team they supported. A stunning, leggy young woman with long black hair broke away from the group, skipping across to deposit double kisses on Marigold and me.

"Victor, *ti omada*?" Poppy asked with a teasing lilt.

"Panathinaikos," I automatically replied, basking in the awareness that the other patrons were impressed that I had been singled out by such a ravishing beauty and that I was up with the Greek lingo.

"Poppy, how delightful to see you. Have you time to join us?" Marigold invited, blushing furiously as Giannis the bee man appeared at Poppy's side.

"Sorry no, we are meeting some friends to watch the match," Poppy said as the handsome couple rushed back to their group after promising to put in an appearance at the baptism party.

"Now that's what I call a nice piece of arm candy," Violet Burke said.

"I can't disagree with you there, Vi," Marigold blushed. Somehow I didn't think they were talking about Poppy.

I may have imagined it, but earlier, when Sandra stopped by to speak to me, I had detected a hint of jealousy in Marigold's demeanour. Yet ironically, when a stunning young woman singled me out, my wife had no problem. I suppose it's because realistically my wife knows that Poppy would never look twice at me, whilst I might be the desperate choice of a bored housewife reduced to reading porn.

The reminder about the UEFA semi-final was timely as in no time at all the whole of the sea-front reverberated with the sound of enthusiastic fans clapping and cheering, urging the Greek side on to unlikely victory. My auspicious choice of venue spared us the ordeal of the televised match, the enthusiasm of the fans fading into background noise. We whiled away a pleasant couple of hours, reluctant to break up our gathering since our table benefited from the occasional welcoming breeze drifting across from the sea. It was only my need for an early night due to my early start repping at Vathia the next day that put an end to our evening.

I remained clueless that Greece had achieved the seemingly impossible and qualified for the final until Sakis filled me in on the great Greek victory the following morning. Naturally, I was filled with *Hellenic* pride in my adopted country.

Chapter 27

Deflecting Attention

Hearing my mother clattering around as she hauled her bulbous form out of bed, I grabbed my coffee and hastily legged it down to the garden for some peace and quiet. After the extremely late return from my guided tour of Vathia the previous day, I needed a strong dose of caffeine in my system before I could cope with Violet Burke. Her presence put the kibosh on my regular early morning routine of sipping coffee on the balcony in blissful solitude, savouring the moment as the village slowly comes to life. Unfortunately the garden was not the oasis of calm that I'd hoped to escape to. Even from a distance, I could hear the sounds of guttural Albanian swearing disturbing the peace.

Tempted though I was to ignore it and take sanctuary in the *apothiki,* I decided to tackle the situation head on. I needed to put a lid on the indecorous commotion before it woke Marigold. It wouldn't do for an unseemly altercation between Guzim and whatever random undesirable he was raging at to put my wife in a bad mood before the baptism. Just to be on the safe side, I armed myself with a trowel, though from the sound of it Guzim appeared to have the upper hand with whomever he was arguing with, not allowing the other fellow to get a word in edgeways.

Rather taken aback to discover the Albanian shed dweller completely alone in the chicken run, railing and shouting at absolutely no one, it crossed my mind that he must be drunk. Perchance my forcing medicinal *ouzo* down his throat had undone the sobriety he had embraced after the birth of his son and heir, Fatos, making him revert to his previous bad habit of breakfast beer.

"Guzim…"

"Koita ton kokoro," Guzim yelled as soon as he spotted me, his voice quavering with outrage as he told me to look at the rooster.

I stared intently at the chicken run, trying to pick out the rooster amongst the chickens. A delicate yellow butterfly chased by Doruntina, Guzim's pet rabbit, seemed to deliberately tease by flitting just out of reach. Raki scampered across the run, dragging its lame leg, before pausing to peck at a grub in the dirt. I could see no sign of the brash and dominant rooster.

"Einai falakros." Telling me it was bald, Guzim pointed to a plump fleshy creature pressed against the netting, only its tell-tale red crown and matching wobbling wattle identifying it as the previously proud cockerel that ruled the roost. Shrunken, shamed and emasculated, the rooster looked as though it had been attacked with a pair of garden shears, only the odd straggly feather still in evidence. Shocked at the sight of the denuded rooster, I tentatively began to ask Guzim if he thought a fox had got in, *"Nomizeis mia alepou…"*

"Mia alepou den to ekana, kapoios to echei mazepsei," Guzim retorted, telling me that a fox

hadn't done that, someone had plucked it.

"Einai kleftis fteron," Guzim shouted. It took me a moment to mentally translate that he had cast the blame on a feather thief.

Experiencing a light-bulb moment, it dawned on me that Violet Burke had almost certainly appropriated the rooster's feathers: I imagined they were probably at this moment adorning her hat.

Thinking aloud, I said, *"To kapelo tis miteras mou."*

"To kapelo tis miteras sou."

"Nai," I confirmed.

At mention of my mother's hat, Guzim shuddered, his anger abating. A coward at heart, the Albanian shed dweller realised he was no match for Violet Burke. Muttering something incomprehensible under his breath, he slunk away, his sulky departure followed by the sound of his moped starting up as he sped off to his labouring job on the coast. I was quite touched by his almost emotional attachment to my rooster.

It appeared that my mother must have taken advantage of my previous day's absence repping at Vathia to get her hands on my rooster. Unless she had drugged the bird, I imagined it must have put up quite a fight. It was definitely a two-person job, yet it struck me as doubtful that Marigold had been complicit in holding the rooster down whilst my mother plucked the best of its feathers in order to embellish her hat. Taking a sip of my coffee, I winced in disgust, the brew now cold. Once again squaring my shoulders, I returned to the house.

"Victor, there you are. I need you to take this trifle over to the taverna now," Marigold greeted me. Amazed that she was up and about so early, I ignored her demand. With my back still turned as I busied myself brewing more coffee, I responded, "Good morning to you too, my darling. It's a beautiful day for the baptism."

"Never mind the weather, Victor. We need to be getting a move on," Marigold said, hysteria creeping into her voice. Finally turning around, I did a double take upon discovering Marigold already done up in her Sunday best.

"Victor, the trifle," my wife reiterated.

"Keep your hat on. What's the rush?" Since my wife was wearing what appeared to be a new hat, I considered my quip quite apt.

"If you'd bothered to come home at a decent hour, you'd know," Marigold fired back in a decidedly aggrieved tone. "Really, Victor, that disappearing act you pulled yesterday was incredibly thoughtless. I must have phoned your mobile at least a dozen times, but did you answer? No. Too busy, off carousing somewhere. If you'd have bothered to keep in contact you would have known that Papas Andreas has been forced to move the baptism forward to 9am. We were lucky he didn't cancel it altogether, he has to shoot off to do a funeral…"

"Anyone we know?"

"No, it's someone in one of the other villages he does his church stuff in."

Relieved that the grim reaper hadn't visited Meli, I launched into an explanation of the previous day's unfortunate events which had left me incommunicado, hurt to the core that my wife could possibly assume the worst.

"Well, for your information I wasn't off carousing."

Marigold at least had the grace to blush when she heard the sorry tale. Returning from Vathia, the tourist coach had suffered a serious mechanical breakdown, leaving us stranded by the side of the road in the middle of nowhere, with no mobile reception. Sakis had nobly volunteered to hike back to Gerolimenos where he phoned the tour company to arrange a replacement coach to come and pick us up, leaving me to entertain a coachload of disgruntled tourists for hours on end.

It was pitch black by the time our alternate transport finally deigned to show up. By then, half of the group were squirming in terror, convinced that we were about to be attacked by marauding pirates who considered a bit of decapitation to be all in a day's work. It seemed that my tales of local history had been a tad too authentic when told in the dark. It was well after midnight when I finally reached home, exhausted, blissfully unaware that the baptism arrangements had undergone a last minute change.

"I should never have assumed you were off gadding…" Marigold began to apologise.

"She thought that you'd gone and taken up with those women from that book club," Violet Burke announced, joining us in the kitchen. "I told her that my Victor doesn't take after his reprobate father…"

"As I recall, you said Victor was probably staying out to get away from my nagging," Marigold interrupted, firing a withering look at my mother.

"Well, you had plenty to say about me driving him away with all the talk of my swollen feet… if you had to live with my feet, you'd go on about them too."

"Clearly, I wasn't avoiding either of you, nor do I have any intention of joining the book club," I said firmly, desperate to put an end to their pointless squabble. "Now, Marigold, you said something about the trifle."

"You need to take the trifle to the taverna then hurry back and change into your suit. We'll meet you in the church," Marigold instructed.

"I'm on it," I promised, grabbing the trifle and heading back out.

To be totally honest, I was in no rush to turn up at church. Having sat through Nikoleta's baptism, I know how these things tend to drag on endlessly. As a non-smoker, I couldn't even use the excuse of slipping out for a crafty cigarette to take a break from the interminable litany intoned in Ancient Greek, an indecipherable language which bore no relation to the Modern Greek language which I still struggle to get to grips with.

With any luck, Nikos would offer me a leisurely coffee when I turned up with the trifle. My stomach rumbled as I looked at the creamy dessert I was carrying, noticing that Marigold had truly surpassed herself. Another groan from my stomach reminded me that not a morsel had passed my lips since yesterday's tourist lunch at Gerolimenos. Perhaps I could persuade Nikos to rustle up some eggs to tide me over.

Sated with coffee and eggs, courtesy of Nikos, I lurked in the church doorway, reluctant to disturb the baptism proceedings by joining my family seated close to the action. Watching Barry and Cynthia hand their precious bundle of joy over to Athena, I guessed that Papas Andreas was about to begin the sacrament: however, I couldn't be certain of what exactly was happening as my view was somewhat obscured by the enormous monstrosity perched on Violet Burke's head. Vibrant red and gold feathers, which only yesterday had graced my rooster, were now prominently displayed on my mother's hat. Presumably superglued to attention, they cut a bizarre image amidst the proliferation of plastic fruit.

Glancing round the church, I realised there were fewer than expected guests in attendance, most likely due to the sudden scheduling change. The seats at the front had been claimed by the coven of Kyria Maria, Kyria Kompogiannopoulou, Litsa and Dina. Despina, the sour, wart-faced old hag from the shop, was planted firmly between Kyria Maria and my mother. I could only presume the miserable shop keeper had gate-crashed, if gate-crashing a public church is an actual thing. Marigold was sitting behind the elderly village ladies with the English contingent of Doreen and Norman, and Edna and Milton. I noticed that Edna was shooting daggers at the back of Violet Burke's head, whilst Milton wriggled uncomfortably beside her. No doubt it would take some time for Edna to overcome her jealousy, no easy task since Violet Burke would certainly be hogging the limelight in that over-the-top hat.

There was no sign of Vi's other admirer, Panos. Like most of the village men, he had made an excuse to duck out of the religious part of the proceedings, though I would put money on the men turning up at the taverna the moment that Nikos unveiled the *ourounopoulo*. There was also no sign of Douglas and family, hardly surprising as they would have had no means of getting to Meli so early. I reflected that it was just as well that the twins were spared the actual ceremony: it would likely have bored them rigid, with not even a hint of gore to amuse them. I hoped that the family managed to make it to the celebration.

My thoughts were interrupted by the sudden sharp cries of Anastasia. I sympathised: I too would be inclined to wail if someone insisted on undressing me in public, rubbing me with oil and water, and immersing me three times in the font. I could see the maternal anguish plastered on Cynthia's face as Papas Andreas passed the now screaming but duly baptised baby into the waiting arms of Athena. As the Papas went through the religious motions of blessing Anastasia's new baptism outfit, I was relieved that my niece was still bald since it spared her the indignity of having three locks of hair cut from her head. I doubt that Andreas is any more skilled with a set of scissors than Apostolos: he has certainly never mastered the art of trimming his unruly beard.

Vangelis and Barry discreetly slipped away from the font, leaving the women to dress the baby. I barely recognised Vangelis, all done up in a stiff and formal suit, befitting his important role as *nonos*.

"*Ela* Victor, join us the outside," Vangelis invited as the two men drew level with me.

"There is the time for the cigarette before the Andreas light the candles."

"Marigold was having kittens when you weren't here when it started," Barry said.

"She's the one who sent me off to the taverna with a trifle," I defended myself. "I didn't want to disturb the baptism by stomping in halfway through."

"At least my sis has got over the hump about not being godmother," Barry revealed.

"How so?" I asked, knowing that Marigold's nose had been pushed out of joint by being relegated to the role of only honorary godmother instead of the real thing.

"Athena explained to her that the actual godparents are expected to take the baby to church for the three consecutive Sundays following the baptism. Marigold said she had no intention of giving up her Sunday lie-ins to bring Anastasia to church."

"Perish the thought," I said, rolling my eyes. Sundays were really no different to any other days of the week when it came to Marigold's lie-ins.

"Marigold said that if she turned up at church for three Sundays in a row, Andreas would be expecting her to be a regular congregant," Barry confided.

"She makes a good point. We both prefer to limit our churchgoing to weddings, baptisms and funerals," I said, thinking we had already gone above and beyond by attending the midnight Greek Saturday service during *Pascha*.

"*Ela* Barry, we're the on again," Vangelis said, tossing his still lit cigarette to the ground and hurrying back inside. Turning to follow, I almost collided with Kyria Maria. The black clad old woman scuttled past me like a sprightly goat, the tell-tale scratches on her hands hinting that she'd been the one to help my mother pluck the rooster. Swooping down, she retrieved Vangelis' discarded cigarette, shoving it greedily between her lips with nary a thought to any concerns about hygiene or possible communicable diseases transferred through spittle.

"*Den ixera oti kapnizes*," I commented, saying I didn't know that she smoked.

"*Mono stin ekklisia*." Drawing the nicotine deep into her lungs, Maria told me that she only smoked in church. Gesticulating expressively, she added with a cackle, "*Ston gio mou aresei poly o ichos tis fonis tou*." Whilst taken aback to hear Maria declare that her son liked the sound of his own voice too much, I had to agree. He was certainly no advocate of a short and snappy religious service. Thinking that perhaps it had slipped his mind that he had a funeral to rush off to, I reflected that since the main participant of the next event wouldn't be in a hurry to go anywhere, Papas Andreas may not feel the need to rush through the baptism and go off and bury him.

Edging my way back into the church, I watched the Papas slip a gold cross and chain around Anastasia's neck. Next he began to light the candles in preparation for what I recalled was the thrice around the font routine, symbolising the baptismal dance of joy. As the congregation began to stand, ready to join in, the peace of the church was rudely shattered by the piercing sound of a siren. As one, the congregation covered their ears, making an unseemly dash for the exit, demanding to know where the fire was.

Barry rushed to guide Cynthia and the baby through the crowd, keenly attempting to protect his baby daughter's ears from the reverberating scream of the siren. Papas Andreas ducked briefly out of sight, returning to view clutching a fire extinguisher. From the corner of my eye, I noticed that Violet Burke hadn't joined the stampede to exit the church. Still in her front row seat, she was desperately rummaging through her handbag, her face scarlet. Marigold reached my side, asking, "What on earth is going on?"

"I've no idea," I lied to my wife, rushing towards Violet Burke. I rather suspected that my mother had somehow managed to trigger her rape alarm.

"I can't turn the damn thing off," my mother shrieked in my ear.

"Allow me," I said, plunging my hand into her handbag and managing, after a bit of fumbling, to silence the blasted contraption.

"I'm that embarrassed," Vi hissed.

"How did you manage to set it off?" I hissed back.

"I was trying to find that sausage roll. I was feeling a bit peckish," Violet Burke admitted, shamefaced. "I must have caught the button on the alarm and it got stuck."

"Best if we don't mention it to anyone, Mother," I hissed back. The last thing I wanted was the local community ostracising my mother: after all, a technical snag could happen to anyone. Reflecting that it may be prudent to deflect attention away from Violet Burke, I approached the Papas.

"I cannot to see the fire," Andreas cried, frantically looking round, poised to unleash the contents of the fire extinguisher.

"I think your mother might have something to do with it. I caught her smoking outside."

Chapter 28

Inextricably Linked

"She's a bonny thing and no mistake. I wouldn't have expected it, considering that Cynthia is no oil painting," Violet Burke said bluntly, watching Cynthia carry Anastasia into the taverna garden.

"Cynthia does have glossy hair," I said in my sister-in-law's defence. "It's too soon to tell if Anastasia will inherit it since she's still bald."

"Aye, you were bald too, lad, she must take after you..."

"I don't think it works like that. My niece isn't a blood relative as such," I pointed out.

"Well, happen you've got enough blood relatives with all of them half-brothers climbing out of the woodwork," Violet Burke said. "I still think that fellow with the yacht would have been a better match."

"You've lost me, Mother."

"That captain bloke with the yacht, Cynthia should have gone for him…"

"It's not a yacht, it's a boat. And Cynthia is happily married to Barry. At least he manages a regular wash."

"I suppose he's scrubbed up quite well today," Violet Burke grudgingly admitted as Barry arrived, flanked by Athena and Vangelis, both looking rather stiff in formal clothing, Athena's hair elaborately coiffed and fixed with spray.

With the baptism brought to an untimely end, we had adjourned to the taverna for the celebratory party. Unfortunately, since the baptism had suffered a scheduling glitch, Nikos wasn't ready for us. When we arrived he was up a ladder outside, attempting to secure the bedraggled sun canopy to an olive tree, or more correctly, the tatty old bed sheet if one was to be pedantic. Nikos complained that Dina hadn't prepared any of the salads yet as she'd insisted on gadding off to church.

"What about the pig?" I asked, looking round in vain since there wasn't even a distant whiff of crackling.

"The cousin second he do the *ourounopoulo* and bring it the noon," Nikos declared. Seeing my look of surprise, he hastily added, "It is not the shop bought inferior rubbish, the cousin he have the pig go the spare."

"Well, I hope that the guests don't descend on my trifle like a pack of locusts," Marigold said, looking at the barren tables. "It's meant to be for dessert, not for elevenses."

"Did someone say elevenses?" Violet Burke piped up.

"There's nothing to eat because we're early," I said. Realising that the Greek contingent of grannies that were filing in didn't understand what I'd said, I helpfully repeated myself in translation, adding that Dina still had to make the salads. *"Den yparchei fagito, eimaste noris. Ntina prepei na ftiaxei tis salates."*

My words galvanised the Greek ladies into action. Rolling their sleeves up, they disappeared into the kitchen, telling Dina they'd give her a hand.

"Don't look at me, I already made the trifle," Marigold said.

"It's a pity Papas Andreas wasn't able to attend," I said.

"Perhaps I should save him a bowl of my trifle. He's quite partial to it."

The British contingent arrived, having stopped off at the village store to splurge on some celebratory fizz.

"Since the shop was all out of champagne, we bought wine," Norman said, showing off half a dozen bottles of cheap plastic plonk.

"Do you think it's a bit early to crack open a bottle?" Doreen asked. The way her fingers were clearly itching to unscrew the nearest bottle made me consider her question rhetorical.

"I could do with a drink," Edna admitted, shooting daggers at my mother whilst keeping a tight hold on Milton's arm. Milton appeared unnaturally subdued, Violet Burke tending to leave him a tad tongue-tied. I had hoped that by now he could manage a better job of hiding the torch he had carried for sixty years.

"It's not even time for elevenses yet," Violet Burke pointed out, rolling her eyes at Edna. Even without the blatant eye roll, I would have surmised that mother had taken a dislike to Edna: I'd never once heard Violet Burke turn down elevenses before, no matter what time of day. As for Milton, mother's eyes passed over him with no sign of recognition. With his usual air of blustery bonhomie suppressed, Milton made such a damp squib of an impression that I doubt Vi even remembered meeting him again the last time she'd visited, let alone exchanging a kiss for a pair of nylons in the Dirty Bird.

"I might as well go and peel some spuds; we'll be needing some chips with the pig," Violet Burke announced before disappearing inside. Unlike Marigold, my mother clearly didn't mind mucking in with the kitchen duties. I may have been tempted to volunteer myself, but I couldn't face the ribbing I knew that I would receive from Nikos for 'doing the woman's work.'

"It may be early, but it is a celebration," Doreen said, giving in to temptation and unscrewing the nearest bottle.

"Don't let Nikos see that shop bought wine, he disapproves of anything but *spitiko,*" I advised.

"He won't have a clue; we'll turn it into punch. We stopped off at ours and raided the cupboards," Doreen said, wielding a bottle of rum, a couple of cans of Fanta *lemoni* and a tin of pineapple chunks.

"I don't know what's got into Doreen. It's not like her to want a drink at this time in the morning. I hope she's not turning into a secret tippler, you know how some of these ex-pats get hooked on morning cocktails," Marigold hissed. "And I hope she isn't entertaining any ideas about making her punch in my trifle bowl."

"I rather think I'd be driven to morning drinking if I was married to Norman," I hissed back, thinking about his endless obsession with traffic cones. Still, it would be worth keeping an eye on Doreen: it wouldn't do for Marigold's closest friend in the village to start emulating Harold.

"I jotted the date down in my diary so that I'll always remember to buy a gift when it is Anastasia's name day," Doreen said, squinting at an old discarded plastic bucket as though it might serve as a suitable receptacle for the punch.

"Anastasia's name day is the 22nd of December," I pointed out. "Greek name days follow the days dedicated to the saint someone is named after, they aren't an anniversary of the baptism date."

"So, was there an actual Saint Anastasia?" Doreen asked, clearly puzzled by this Greek concept.

"Indeed. Agia Anastasia the Pharmakolitria. She is the patron saint of poisons…"

"You and your poisons, Victor," Marigold laughed. "Perhaps we should have another discussion about digging up the oleanders. It would be dreadful if little Anastasia was struck down by a poisonous substance in our garden when she's named after the saint of poisons."

"It would be a terrible irony," I agreed.

Excusing myself, I wandered over to join Barry. My brother-in-law was making a rather ineffectual job of concealing himself behind an olive tree.

Grabbing hold of my arm, Barry hissed, "Squeeze in next to me, I'm trying to avoid Athena. She is determined to school me in every last obscure baptism practice."

"But the baby has already been baptised," I pointed out. I presumed that Barry would be safely off Athena's hook now that the churchly bit was over with.

"It doesn't end there. Athena is insisting that we don't bathe the baby for the next three days. She says it's tradition. Little Ana loves bath time; you should see the way she gurgles," Barry sighed, a wistful look on his face.

"Oh well, look on the bright side. At least Athena is now obligated to buy Anastasia a new pair of shoes every Easter," I said.

"She's not even crawling yet, never mind needing shoes for walking."

"Still a new pair of shoes every Easter is not to be sniffed at. Shoes aren't cheap, you know. I went through a small fortune in shoe leather for Benjamin."

"Well, I just hope Athena doesn't spring any more baptismal surprises on me," Barry sighed. "That was a right song and dance in the church. I think it would have dragged on forever if that fire alarm hadn't gone off."

"It wasn't a fire alarm. Keep this to yourself, Barry, but it was Violet Burke's rape alarm going off in her handbag..."

"Oh my God, what's she like? Does she really think she's in danger of..."

"No, of course not. She brought it for the goats," I said, hoping Barry caught my drift. "If anyone mentions the alarm..."

"Don't worry; I'll say it was a car alarm. I owe your mum a drink for cutting the proceedings short," Barry snorted. As Cynthia approached with the baby, he added, "Mum's the word."

As I reached out to take the baby for a cuddle, Cynthia said, "Marigold has just told me that the saint that Anastasia is named after is the patron saint of poisons. It sent a shiver down my spine when I heard it, I'd no idea. I do hope it's not a bad omen."

"Superstitious twaddle," Barry snorted. "Did you hear Athena laying down the law that we mustn't bathe the baby for the next three days?"

"She must be mad if she thinks I'd deprive this little sweetheart of bath time," Cynthia said defiantly. "She adores bath time."

"And when she has her first post-baptismal bath in three days' time, we are meant to water the flowers with her bathwater," Barry continued.

"Well, I do that anyway. There is a severe water shortage, you know," Cynthia replied.

Noticing that Milton had managed to shake off his clingy wife, I handed the baby back to Cynthia and made my way over.

"I say, old chap, jolly good punch. Have you tried it?" Milton asked, prising a pineapple chunk from between his teeth.

"I was hoping to have a quiet word, Milton."

"That sounds ominous…"

"Not at all. I happened to run into some ladies down on the coast the other evening. They are members of an ex-pat book club and they've only selected 'Delicious Desire' as their book of the month," I revealed.

"I say, old chap, that's a bit…I'm lost for words."

"It is excellent news. I expect you'll soon be getting your hands on some royalty cheques," I said.

"Did they happen to mention if they were enjoying it?" Milton asked.

"A couple of them certainly sang your porn's praises," I said, wondering if I should mention it hadn't been everyone's cup of tea. A vision of Bessie's smug face swam before my eyes and I decided the opinion of the insufferable woman counted for nothing. She'd struck me as far too opinionated for her own good, with her ludicrous aspirations to turn out the next Booker prize winner after absorbing the contents of a 'how to write a novel' manual.

"Erotica, old chap, erotica," Milton barked.

"I think you may have even inspired a couple of them to spice up things in the bedroom. If I know anything about women, I'm sure they'll be recommending it to all their friends," I said.

"Couldn't have done it without you, old chap. Your advice was invaluable."

"Nonsense," I protested, feeling a tad guilty that I'd spurned Milton's constant efforts to persuade me to give it the once over.

"Hardly nonsense, old chap. Without your sound advice, I would have shelled out a fortune on one of those rip off vanity publishers. You steered me right, telling me not to pay to have it published."

"That's true," I said, accepting credit where credit was due.

"You don't suppose Violet Burke might like a copy?"

"Absolutely not. My mother has the tact of a fishwife. In no time at all your cover as Scarlett Bottom would be well and truly blown."

"Ah, quite, got to preserve the old anonymity and all that. Whatever you think best, old chap. Think I'll just grab another glass of punch. My book being the book club choice deserves a toast, what."

Delighted to spot the arrival of Douglas and his family, I rushed over to greet them. "You made it."

"Can you believe that the owner of the hotel

we're staying in offered to drive us up when she heard that we were missing a family celebration? It was so kind of her," Elaine gushed.

"And she's going to collect us later. Wouldn't take no for an answer, absolutely insisted," Douglas said.

"It's a taste of *philoxenia,* genuine Greek hospitality," I said, happy that the family had experienced it first-hand.

Marigold joined us and we made arrangements to meet up the following day for some family beach time before the coach arrived early evening to take them to the airport. As we discussed plans to meet up again in the future, my attention was distracted by the arrival of a battered old van. Nikos called over, telling me and Barry to give him a hand with the pig.

It took all our combined strength to manoeuvre the deliciously aromatic whole roast suckling pig from the back of the van and put it in pride of place on the table. Nikos' second cousin had certainly outdone himself, his skill with the spit having produced tender and moist pork beneath an exquisite layer of glistening crackling, all without sticking the proverbial apple in its mouth. Its arrival was followed by a flurry of activity as the Greek ladies emerged from the kitchen weighed down with a tempting array of salads and dips to accompany the pig. I couldn't help but smile at what appeared to be a new development: Violet Burke and Dina talking at each other over a vast platter of chips. Perhaps my brilliant idea that Violet Burke could occupy herself with some work in the taverna would prove to have legs after all.

The smell of the *ourounopoulo* appeared to magically conjure the presence of the village men. Spiros arrived, having missed the baptism because of the funeral. With Sampaguita on his arm, my friend looked happier than I'd seen him for months: in fact he was positively glowing, as was his fragrant Filipina flower. Spiros was closely followed by Giannis and Poppy, Panos and Mathias. Even Dimitris showed his face, though naturally he made it clear he would scarper once the music started. Whilst the men made a beeline for the food, the Greek ladies who had congregated in the kitchen swooped on the baby, admiring the beautiful christening outfit handcrafted by Kyria Maria. In no time at all they were busy attempting to swaddle Anastasia in an assortment of knitted blankets, determined she wouldn't come down with a chill. Did I mention the noontime temperature was close to 36 degrees in the shade?

Leaving Violet Burke to talk at her new-found Greek friends, I grabbed a seat at a table with Marigold, Barry, Spiros and Sampaguita. Barry, desperate to put some distance between himself and Athena, in case the new godmother tried to school him in yet more baptismal related customs, persuaded Cynthia that it was her turn to be on the receiving end of being bossed. Rolling her eyes at her husband, Cynthia decreed, "Athena and Vangelis are family now, get used to it."

As Marigold spooned some rich green *horta* onto my plate, I couldn't resist reminding her that the summer dish was prepared from *vlita*. Ignoring me, she turned to Barry, complaining that he really ought to have invited Sherry since Mathias was here.

"Why he should to invite the Sherry?" Spiros interjected. "I hear she not like to, how you to say in the English, hob the nob with the help."

"That's as maybe, but I was hoping to fix Sherry up with a local man and she seemed to be quite taken with Mathias…in spite of his proclivity for eating raw garlic," Marigold said.

"She did stay on when we left Apostolos' name day party," I agreed, thinking perhaps

Marigold's matchmaking efforts hadn't been a dismal failure for once.

"The Mathias has not been the strong of the late and he worry about the becoming the burden on the sister Litsa," Spiros confided in a loud voice. "I think he may to show the interest in the Sherry for the help in the home, like the Sampaguita do for the uncle."

"Hey, Spiro," Nikos called out. "I to overhear you. The Mathias he say he suppose a wife would cost the less money than paying the woman to come in to the help."

"Thank goodness Nikos didn't blurt that out in Greek," Marigold said, clearly mortified.

"The food is wonderful," Barry exclaimed, piling *skordalia* onto a piece of crusty bread.

"The cousin second do the excellent *ourounopoulo*," Nikos agreed. "But why your friends the British take that disgusting drink from the bowel instead of to drink the *spitiko*?"

"Bowl," I automatically corrected, thinking I must remember to ask Kyria Kompogiannopoulou how she got on at the hospital with her bladder. Whilst I hoped she spared me the gory details, it would only be polite to enquire. "And the disgusting drink is punch."

"Punch, what is the punch?" Nikos demanded.

Clueless, I whipped out my handy English to Greek pocket dictionary to proffer a ready translation.

"Einai grothia."

"I think you to need the new dictionary," Spiros said between snorts of laughter.

"Or more the Greek lessons," Vangelis joined in.

"Why, what have I gone and said wrong now?" I asked.

"The *grothia* is the..." Spiros demonstrated by punching me hard in the arm.

"I'm going to have to go back and change my shoes, my feet are so swollen they'll likely explode if I try a bop," Violet Burke informed me when Nikos gave in to popular demand and produced his *bouzouki.*

"I'll walk you back, Mother," I offered.

"No need to bother, lad."

"It's no bother. Here, take my arm; it might ease some of the pressure on your feet."

Strolling back to the house, I could feel the weight of Violet Burke's bulk pulling me down. She was certainly suffering with her swollen feet much more than she had on previous visits, her wheezing testimony that the short walk was a strain. Nearing the house, I decided it was time to broach the subject of her living arrangements. Steering her into the downstairs storage, I suggested she take a breather in the cool surroundings.

Creaking ominously, the deckchair sagged as she sank her bulbous form with a weary sigh.

"Happen that doctor has a point about my weight; I might have to give some serious consideration to giving up chips."

"There's always moderation instead of abstinence," I suggested.

"That wife of yours has been putting ideas in your head. There's nowt going on between me and Panos," Vi asserted.

Baffled by her protestation, I must confess to being a tad slow on the uptake.

"I meant you could eat chips in moderation, rather than give them up entirely," I clarified when the penny dropped.

"Happen it will be easier to cut down when I have to stop working in the chippy. Why've you dragged me in here, Victor?" Vi asked, looking around with interest.

"We've been thinking of converting this space into a separate abode, something like a granny flat. Marigold and I were rather hoping that you may consider living in it, part of the year, at least. I don't like to think of you in a high-rise. This is on street level so it would be easy on your feet."

For once my mother was silent, her face inscrutable as she gave the *apothiki* the once over.

"You'd have your work cut out. It's just a mucky storage dump."

"It won't be when Barry and Vangelis work their magic. Look past the filth and clutter," I implored, using all my strength to prise open the old, stiff wooden shutters. As they gave way with a creak in need of a good oiling, natural light flooded the area, highlighting dust motes and spiders scurrying into the corners.

"Look how thick these stone walls are, they keep the place cool. And there's a lovely curve to the ceiling."

"Has it even got a lav?" the ever practical Vi asked.

"We'll have a bathroom fitted, with a bath if you like. We could put a nice bedroom in the back and your sitting room would overlook the street. Marigold is full of ideas for décor."

"You don't want me under your feet."

"We do…I mean you won't be," I insisted, a tad confused. Violet Burke would literally be under my feet if she lived down here, without getting under my feet in the conventional sense. "You like it over here, don't you?"

"Well, it takes a bit of getting used to, with it being foreign and all, but I do like to come over to see you…"

"And you're making some good friends locally," I encouraged. "You get on like a house on fire with Maria."

"It's handy her being so welcoming. It keeps me from getting under your feet all day."

About to protest, I kept schtum, realising she was only reiterating the points which Marigold and I had discussed. I decided to listen and let Violet Burke have her say.

"I'd come to terms with abandoning you, Victor. When I see how you've turned out, it makes me that proud. To be honest, it might have been a different story if I'd kept you, there's no denying that. Finding you after all these years turned my world upside down, I have to admit, and you've done nothing but make me feel like part of the family. Even that wife of yours has her moments."

"You are part of the family," I said honestly.

"I've just been plodding on, never thinking things would change. After seeing off the last of four husbands, I wasn't up for more upheaval. I expected to work in the chippy till I dropped…coming out here to see you gave me something to look forward to."

"You'd rather sit around drinking tea with Maria than with Edna Billings, even if she does leave the twigs in it. And you could always bring a suitcase of Tetley over," I said, hoping my powers of persuasion did the trick.

"I don't traipse all the way out here at my age for the tea, Victor. I come to Greece to see you. To make up for all those lost years without the son I abandoned. Do you know, the first time I came over, I thought you'd most likely disown me, thinking me an embarrassment."

About to deny it, my face reddened as I recalled my first meeting with Violet Burke. I vividly remembered I had indeed considered it a total embarrassment to be the spawn of the bulbous overdone creature that had burst into my dinner party with all the grace of a bull in a china shop. I could still picture the pity on Barry's face when it dawned on him that the vulgar harridan was indeed the callous absconded parent who had abandoned me as a baby in a bucket at the railway station. I recalled the personal anguish I had suffered as I tried to come to terms with the situation, all the time instinctively knowing that there was no doubt that Violet Burke was my mother and that our lives would be inextricably linked from that moment.

"You've grown on me, Mother," I said.

"Like fungus, lad." In spite of her quip, Vi's voice was filled with gruff affection as she reached over to take my hand. Whilst this may have seemed like an opportune moment for us to admit that we had grown fond of each other, neither of us were the type for emotional declarations.

"You'll think on it then?"

"I will, Victor. I'll give it some thought."

Chapter 29

Are We Greek, Now?

"Goodbye, Uncle Bucket, goodbye, Aunty Bucket," the twins cheerily cried as the coach pulled away, waving vigorously until they were out of sight.

"It's just the two of us again," Marigold said wistfully.

"Well, three if you count my mother," I pedantically pointed out.

"I think we can say that we lucked out with our new relatives, I'm delighted to call them family," Marigold said, tucking her arm in mine as we strolled at a leisurely pace towards the seafront.

"Even Violet Burke," I teased.

"Yes, even your mother. I have to admit she's growing on me..."

"In small doses," I finished her sentence.

Having both immensely enjoyed the visit of Douglas and his family, we were sad to see them go. Fortunately, we knew there would be plenty of opportunity in the future to make up for lost time.

"Kyria Maria will be relieved to get her tortoise back. She is so attached to it," Marigold sighed. "She was quite distraught when she couldn't find it this morning. I know she can be an utter pest, but I must admit to feeling quite sorry for her."

"I'll sneak it back over the wall as soon as we get back to Meli," I promised, swinging the carrier bag containing Maria the tortoise, previously known as *Frappé*. "I can't believe the twins were audacious enough to think they could smuggle a tortoise back to England in Douglas' suitcase."

"Or how they were bold enough to snatch it in the first place." Marigold shook her head, still barely able to credit the twins' mischievous antics. "They certainly fooled me by saying they wanted to slip out of the party to say goodbye to the chickens."

"Not only did they get clean away with the tortoise, they managed to successfully secrete it in the hotel overnight," I said, marvelling at their ingenuity.

"At least you discovered it before they got it up to the airport," Marigold said.

"I thought it a tad suspicious the way Douglas' shirts appeared to have a life of their own," I said. "It's a good job I spotted something amiss: it might have been a goner after the coach trip. I doubt Douglas' case is equipped with ventilation holes."

"It must be illegal to attempt to smuggle a tortoise through customs. It's bad enough suffering the stigma of a dead father-in-law with a prison record, without our new nieces joining the criminal ranks."

"The Greeks are very fond of children though, I doubt they would have thrown them in a cell," I reassured my wife.

"I should hope not."

As the darkness closed in, a slight breeze stirred. We inhaled the heady scent of Angel's

Trumpets, almost overpowering the more delicate fragrance of bougainvillea. Rounding the corner, the lights of the coastal resort twinkled brightly outside the restaurants and café bars, cries of excitement reaching our ears.

"Gosh, it sounds busy down here tonight," Marigold said.

"Hardly surprising. It's the football final and Greece is playing."

"There'll be a lot of bad tempered Greeks about tomorrow when they lose," Marigold laughed.

"A miracle may happen and they may be victorious," I chortled. "I hope they do, I seem to recall Barry stands to win a fair sum from his wager. Let's find a quiet spot to enjoy a glass of wine."

"Not for you, Victor. It's your turn to be the designated driver."

"When isn't it?" I quipped.

Finding a quiet spot overlooking the bay, we whiled away a pleasant evening, sipping our drinks and watching the waves lap onto the beach. I reflected that life couldn't get much better than this. Up-sticking to Greece had closed one door behind us, but new doors were opening, promising wonderful days ahead, days that would be enriched by our growing circle of family and friends.

The peace of the moment was disturbed by euphoric cheers, the air carrying them like a wave.

"You don't suppose…"

"I rather believe Greece may have achieved the impossible and triumphed in the football," I said.

Caught up in the palpable sense of excitement, Marigold took my hand, her voice quavering with pride as she whispered, "That's our country."

"Do you think we could start calling ourselves Greek then, instead of European residents?"

A Note from Victor

All Amazon reviews most welcome.

Please feel free to drop a line if you would like information on the release date of future volumes in the Bucket series at
vdbucket@gmail.com

Printed in Great Britain
by Amazon